W9-ABN-524

The publisher gratefully acknowledges the generous support of the Higher Education Endowment Fund of the University of California Press Foundation, which was established by a major gift from the Atkinson Family Foundation.

Dynamics of the
Contemporary University

Dynamics of the Contemporary University

GROWTH, ACCRETION,
AND CONFLICT

NEIL J. SMELSER

UNIVERSITY OF CALIFORNIA PRESS
Berkeley   Los Angeles   London

CENTER FOR STUDIES IN HIGHER EDUCATION
Berkeley

The Center for Studies in Higher Education at the University of
California, Berkeley, is a multidisciplinary research and policy center
on higher education oriented to California, the nation, and comparative international issues. CSHE promotes discussion among university
leaders, government officials, and academics; assists policy making by
providing a neutral forum for airing contentious issues; and keeps the
higher education world informed of new initiatives and proposals. The
Center's research aims to inform current debate about higher education
policy and practice.

University of California Press, one of the most distinguished university presses in the United States, enriches lives around the world by
advancing scholarship in the humanities, social sciences, and natural
sciences. Its activities are supported by the UC Press Foundation and by
philanthropic contributions from individuals and institutions. For more
information, visit www.ucpress.edu.

University of California Press
Berkeley and Los Angeles, California

University of California Press, Ltd.
London, England

Library of Congress Cataloging-in-Publication Data

Smelser, Neil J.
  Dynamics of the contemporary university : growth, accretion, and
conflict / Neil J. Smelser.
     pages cm
  ISBN 978-0-520-27581-2 (hardback)
  1. Universities and colleges—United States. 2. Universities and
colleges—Administration—United States. 3. Educational change—
United States. I. Title.
  LA227.4.S581   2013
  378.73—dc23   2012039812

Manufactured in the United States of America
22 21 20 19 18 17 16 15 14 13
10 9 8 7 6 5 4 3 2 1

In keeping with a commitment to support environmentally responsible
and sustainable printing practices, UC Press has printed this book
on Rolland Enviro 100, a 100% post-consumer fiber paper that is FSC
certified, deinked, processed chlorine-free, and manufactured with
renewable biogas energy. It is acid-free and EcoLogo certified.

Contents

Acknowledgments

I send thanks and bouquets to the Center for Studies in Higher Education, University of California, Berkeley—sponsors of the Clark Kerr Lectures—both for doing me the honor of selecting me in the first place and for facilitating all my preparatory efforts for the lectures. Jud King, director of the center, was supportive and helpful both formally and informally, as was John Douglass, senior research fellow. Rondi Phillips, staff member at the center, gracefully handled all logistics, right up to the point of equipping me properly with microphones at the lectures. Steven Brint, fellow sociologist and vice provost for undergraduate education at UC Riverside, guaranteed that my delivery of the third lecture on that campus was a successful occasion. I would also like to thank Ziza Delgado, my long-standing and flawless research assistant, for locating and interpreting empirical materials on selected trends in higher education. The staff of the Education-Psychology Library on the Berkeley campus was, as always, cheerfully accommodating in my bibliographical searching. Finally, I am most grateful to colleagues, friends, and curious others for coming to my lectures in impressive numbers, for their evident interest in what I had to say, and for helping me with apt and sophisticated questions and observations after each lecture.

ONE Dynamics of American Universities

It is a custom on this occasion to honor the figure for whom these lectures are named and to acknowledge how deeply honored I am to have been chosen to deliver them. I do both these things, not out of the pressure of ceremony, but from the heart. Clark Kerr was (and is) such an important part of my own career that I must add a personal note.

I met Clark Kerr in 1958, about two weeks after I arrived on the Berkeley campus as a new assistant professor. He, as new President, and Glenn Seaborg, as new Chancellor, had invited faculty appointees to a welcoming social occasion. We merely shook hands at the time, and to him I was a face in the crowd, but I knew of his heroics in the loyalty-oath crisis years earlier. I could not have known that in the coming decade he would lead California into its magnificent Master Plan, enunciate his historic conception of the multiversity, ride herd over multiple crises in the 1960s, establish his presidency as a legendary one, and become the century's leading spokesman for higher education.

In the following decade I myself was drawn into campus affairs in such a way that Kerr came to notice me, and he invited me to join the Technical Advisory Committee of his Carnegie Commission on Higher Education. There I, along with Martin Trow, Sheldon Rothblatt, Bud Cheit, and Fred Balderston, came to constitute a group that I called "Clark's boys." My relationship with Clark was cemented in those years, and he sought my advice on diverse matters, and ultimately my help with his memoirs. Clark Kerr and I would meet in the Clark Kerr Room of the Men's Faculty Club, sit under the portrait of Clark Kerr, and I would always order the Clark Kerr Special from the menu, even when I didn't like the plate. It was a humbling honor when Clark invited me to write the foreward to *The Gold and the Blue* (Kerr 2001; Kerr 2003) from a crowd of much more visible and notable candidates. I apologize for this too-personal introduction, but I felt it important to reveal the depth of memories and feelings I have on this occasion.

APOLOGIA

I now offer another apology, this on how I am going to proceed. In covering the recent literature on higher education, reading the press, and conversing with colleagues and friends, I get a picture of urgency and crisis. We are being starved by the public and the politicians, tenure is disappearing with the proletarianization of the academic labor force, the idea of the university is being eroded by the forces of the market and corporatization, and we are being threatened by the spectacular growth of online, for-profit organizations of questionable quality.

I know these questions are on your minds as well, and I feel the pressure to put my two cents' worth on these overwhelming issues right away. In the context of such urgency, it is almost a matter for personal guilt if I don't. I can assure you that I will comment, but not right away, not from the hip, and not in the language of the day. If I did so, I am confident I would add nothing to the babble of voices. As an alternative, I am going to try to elucidate a few first principles about the nature of higher education (especially the university), particularly about its change and stability. So, in the first chapter I will develop some principles about change in higher education, using historical and contemporary examples. In the second I will trace some of the endless ramifications of these principles. And in the third—using the foregoing analyses—I will develop assessments and conditional predictions about higher education's major contemporary problems as they are superimposed on its structural history.

One final apology: my academic career has been that of a social scientist, or more precisely a sociologist afflicted with an incurable interdisciplinary impulse. I have also had a lifetime of immersion in my university's departmental, administrative, and academic senate affairs. Such diversity of experience often produces eclectic, contingent outlooks. But here my approach will be primarily that of a sociologist. In particular, I will be guided by the idea of a *social system*. This stress has weakened in the social sciences in the past several decades, along with the atrophy of interest in social theory in general, but it is clearly relevant to the study of higher education. Elsewhere I have argued (Smelser 2001: xx–xxi) that some of Clark Kerr's extraordinary success as chancellor and president could be assigned to his understanding of the "systemness" of his university—the intricate relations among its many parts and its relations to its environments.

By "system" I mean an entity with identifiable but interrelated parts, such that changes in one part influence the other parts and the entity as a whole. The campus-based college or university, with its departments, schools, layers of administration, and support systems—to say nothing of its array of internal constituencies—is surely a system. So is a multicampus system, though perhaps in a looser sense. And so is higher education as a whole, with its differentiated segments and types of institutions. The notion of *open system* gives importance to forces external to it. The idea of system also equips one with tools to analyze the ramifications of discrete changes and their consequences. Finally, a system perspective permits us to generate new insights about many murkier, evasive aspects of our history and our contemporary situation. In addition to this stress, I will make extensive use of the concepts of culture (including subculture), social structure, and groups and group conflict, all standard items in the sociological repertoire. Finally, however, to understand higher education and its dynamics, one must—and I will— selectively bring in tools and insights from economics, history, political science, anthropology, and psychology.

I might cite a final advantage of thinking systemically about higher education. We know so much and we say so much about the characteristics, the history, the nature, and the problems of higher education that our minds are in danger of being overloaded. We academics are great observers, talkers, writers, and worriers; our stock-in-trade is words and insights. This brings to mind the anecdote about a committee meeting at which the chair confidently states that he thinks the group has come to closure on an issue, but one committee member objects and says, "But we haven't said everything that's ever been said on the subject." I do not threaten to do that, but by appealing to the idea of system I hope modestly to make a few new *connections* between known or asserted things. Why, for example, is it that higher education is simultaneously known to be an institution with a history of spectacular growth and solid institutionalization *and* simultaneously proclaimed to be in crisis or doomed (Birnbaum and Shushok 2001)? Why are our universities so admired and emulated abroad and so bashed within our boundaries? Why are universities and kindred institutions, so splendid and serene in hope and theory, also fraught with internal ambivalence and group conflict? In these chapters I hope to make some sense of these and other questions.

WHAT KIND OF CREATURE IS HIGHER EDUCATION?

I begin not with a formal definition of higher education but a listing of its most salient characteristics as a social institution—characteristics essential for the analysis presented in these chapters.

Functions

Describers, apologists, advocates, commentators, and historians of higher education often list a number of its functions, almost all positive. There is variation but some consensus on the following in the literature:

- To preserve, create, advance and transmit knowledge to the young, who will be future professional, political, and business leaders of society.

- To impart ranges of expertise to those who will be leaders.

- To serve society more directly by providing useful knowledge for economic growth and prosperity, and community development (Trani and Holsworth 2010).

- To foster individual achievement, social mobility, equality of opportunity, and social justice.

- To serve democracy further by improving the literacy, knowledge, rationality, tolerance and fair-mindedness, and responsible participation on the part of citizens. This has served as a main buttressing argument for liberal and general education.

- To preserve, develop, and augment the general cultural values of our civilization, both by cultivating those values among the young and honing of them through constant and responsible criticism.

- At a different level, to come to the assistance of the nation in its vital struggles—for example, wars, international political competition, and heightened economic competition associated with globalization (Duderstadt 2000).

The Problematic Status of "Functions"

This list is fair enough. However, I have come to regard this kind of presentation as problematical in some respects. I list my reservations:

- The exact conceptual status of these activities as "functions" is unclear. They may be regarded as descriptions of what institutions *accomplish*; they may be regarded as ideals or goals for which they *strive* but attain only partially; they may be regarded as a source of cultural *legitimacy* for institutions of higher education, which, like all institutions, require such legitimacy to secure their place, their support, and their continuity in society; or finally and more cynically, they may be regarded as a form of *advocacy*—namely, as claims to prestige and status, ploys in seeking support, or intellectualized defenses by spokesman in institutions under attack. They are all these things, of course, but the multiple connotations make for ambiguity and perhaps conflict with respect to the status and meaning of the claimed functions.

- Insofar as they are claimed to describe what educational institutions do, they involve *causal claims*—that is to say, usually implicit assertions that certain lines of activity (teaching, conducting research, advising governments) actually have the intended, usually positive effects. These claims are difficult if not impossible to establish definitively or scientifically. All that we know from evaluation research on "results of schooling," "educational impact," and the general relations between knowledge and policy demonstrates that multiple variables are at work and that it is extremely difficult to establish reliable relationships between intervention and outcome, even though elaborate quasi-experimental efforts to control the effects of contaminating variables are made (Rossi and Freeman 1992).

- It follows that there is inevitably a residue of generalized *faith* that the activities of institutions of higher education are fulfilling their functions adequately or fully. Moreover, this faith usually is not automatically granted and therefore rests on shakier grounds than in other areas (health, protecting the nation, and sufficiency in agriculture) in which the goals are matters of vital importance and high consensus.

As a result of these difficulties in describing abstract functions, I am going to view the "functions" of higher education more concretely and historically—namely, as sequence of "compacts" between agencies *outside* those institutions (states, the federal government, philanthropists and donors, interested commercial and industrial parties, and a real and imagined "public"). For example, Thelin concludes that "federal government support for higher education displays a distinctive characteristic: it often is a convenient means for the U.S. government to attain larger national goals" (2004b: 37). States are interested in the correlations between the proportion of their students enrolled in higher education and their rate of economic growth (Zumeta 2004)—even though the direction of causality may be questionable. Actually, the relationship is more complex; it is one of mutual opportunism. External persons or agencies perceive an opportunity, a belief that higher education is a valuable asset in pursuing one or more of their purposes, and educational institutions accept these offers opportunistically. Or, if they are more proactive, those institutions invent and seek out new functions as a way of enhancing their competitive position and survival.

The "compacts" emerging from these relationships are typically *not* strict contracts in the legal sense of goods or services being delivered for specific consideration. State governments expect that state colleges and universities will serve mainly the citizens of the state, and those institutions generally comply. Colleges and universities use philanthropic donations for designated purposes, but they resist conditions of regulation by donors, delivery of specific services, and guarantee of specific "outcomes." Academic freedom is granted with implicit expectations that academics will not exploit the privilege or behave in uncivil ways. Correspondingly, these compacts have had mainly *generalized* expectations, unspoken assumptions, and trust.

We may say at this early moment, then, that even at the most fundamental level institutions of higher education, both in their functions and in their relations with external agencies, exhibit notable levels of ambiguity, nonspecificity, and taken-for-grantedness. In my estimation these have been great institutional advantages for colleges and universities, essential for their freedom, autonomy, and adaptability. Yet those very qualities of vagueness increase the probabilities of misunderstandings, disappointments, conflicts, ex post facto accusations of promises made but not kept, as well as recriminations and defenses against those recriminations. The functions I have identified—what society has asked of higher education—do not guarantee such outcomes, but they tilt the system in the direction of producing them.

Moral Embeddedness

Cutting across these functional linkages between higher education and society is one final fundamental characteristic. Education in general and higher education in particular are inevitably matters of *moral* concern. This is grounded in two circumstances. First, all education is directly involved in the institutionalization, reproduction, and transmission of the fundamental values of society to succeeding generations—always a moral matter. Second, the historical heritage of higher education is profoundly moral. From their medieval beginnings, its activities were indistinguishable from religious morality. This translated itself to the view of the university as a *sacred* entity, and, for its members, the idea that involvement in the university represented a higher religious *calling*. Even though most universities have been "de-churched" (Tuchman 2009) and are by now fully secular institutions, versions of the sacred, ecclesiastical hierarchy and the calling survive in recognizable form (see Brubacher 1978). Brint recently observed that "[e]ducation is as close to a secular religion as we have in the United States" (2011: 2). In modern garb this includes the ideas that education's work is of the highest value (example: "The university preserves and interprets the best of what human intelligence has created and written" [Hearn 2006: 160]); that that work demands love; and that educators should manifest a certain ascetic, antimaterialistic attitude (which conveys further that one should not want and/or become too involved in worldly rewards). These ideals are held, in variable form and strength, by those *in* the academy and as expectations for the academy on the part of those *outside* it. The three basic historical roles of higher education—teaching, search for knowledge, and service to society—are each endowed with the connotation that they are publicly valued missions. Part—but only part—of the claims of higher education to status, public support, and legitimacy is a matter of representing itself and being regarded by outsiders as a *higher* activity, no longer fully priestly but having some of those qualities and roles.

Three corollaries follow from the postulate that institutions of higher education are seats of claims to and recognition of high moral purpose:

First, claims to a morality (and special expertise) generate special and high *expectations*, both within the academy and in the larger public. If a class of activities is designated as special and superior, those practitioners of them are expected to live up to those standards. This has been a constant characteristic of priestly and quasi-priestly classes—the pressure to live up to their billing.

Second, on the basis of such claims, academic classes are typically granted *high status* and do not hesitate to accept and claim that status. Nor do they hesitate to grant others less status. Balderston argued that "administrative staff members, including those at professional and senior levels, cannot share directly in this [academic] status system and are, worse yet, sometimes the victims of academic snobbery and contempt for bureaucracy" (1974: 80). Duderstadt, himself a long-serving president in a leading university, commented simply that "[academic] arrogance knows no bounds" (2000: 123).

Third, an inevitable ingredient that accompanies claims to moral commitment, high expectations, and high status is that *deviation* from its standards is more than simple straying. It is tinged with the corruption of the sacred, and thus justifies strong moral reactions. Consistently, the preferred mode of reflecting and writing on colleges and universities has been one of morality and moral passion. Colleges and universities embody the highest of hopes and the greatest of despair, blame, and moral loss when these hopes seem to be compromised. That language is infused with the positive affects of love, admiration, and rhapsody and the negative affects of disappointment, betrayal, and outrage. With all this the stage is set for recurrent episodes of both idealization and vilification.

I hope that these general reflections will prove useful in enlightening the endemic conflicts that swirl around processes of change in academia (below, pp. 60–64). But I do not wish to press these observations too far and claim that the moral dimension is the sole or strongest ingredient of higher education; secular elements abound in academic culture. But it cannot be ignored as a heritage and a reality, and if we do not keep it in mind, we cannot understand what has transpired and is transpiring.

The peculiarities I have identified—functions, relations with society, and moral embeddedness—supply the context for the topics to which I now turn: growth and change in American higher education. In fact, that process of growth itself is a distinctive feature of higher education. But that growth, to be understood, has to be regarded in relation the heritage of societal involvement and moral embeddedness.

STRUCTURAL CHANGES ACCOMPANYING GROWTH

Growth has been the hallmark of American higher education in the past one and one-half centuries. This has been pulsating, to be sure, with periods of extremely rapid increase in, for example, the late nineteenth century and the two decades following World War II, as well as periods of stagnation such as Great Depression and the 1970s and 1980s. We will examine the causes and consequences of such irregularities as we go along, but initially we must clear some theoretical ground.

One way of tracking growth is by different quantitative indices— expenditures, numbers of students, faculty, graduates, and institutions. These reveal its magnitude. However, social scientists know that neither rapid nor long-term growth typically occurs without some qualitative changes in the *social structures* involved in that growth. The following are some typical structural processes.

Increasing the Size of Units

Much population growth—that associated with increases in fertility— occurs through the increasing size of families, among other changes. While this may entail changes in intrafamily dynamics, it does not directly produce structures *other* than the family. In higher education we observe the same principle—for example, in campus policies of expanding enrollment of students and size of faculty in the face of increasing demand. Increases in size typically create some economies of scale but sooner or later reach a limit and generate pressures for other kinds of structural change.

Segmentation of Units

Segmentation is a form of change that is also relatively simple in that it involves the increase of identical or similar units. It is another structural concomitant of population change—namely, the multiplication of family units without significant structural changes in family structure. Another example is an automobile manufacturer's decision to increase the number of retail outlets in response to augmented demand. The rapid increase in numbers of four-year and community colleges between 1950 and 1970 is an example from higher education, as is the increase in numbers of for-profit distance-learning institutions in recent decades.

Differentiation

Differentiation is one of the most widespread structural concomitants of growth and efficiency. It is the principle in Adam Smith's formula of the division of labor (specialization) leading to greater productivity and wealth—a formula he associated explicitly with growth. Whole institutions can also become more specialized as well. Much of the story of the Western family during the history of industrialization, for example, was its *loss* of functions as a productive economic unit (wage labor outside the family accomplished that), as a welfare system (the growth of public welfare accomplished that), as an instrumental training ground (mass primary and secondary education accomplished that), and as a principal agency for sustaining the aged (social-security systems accomplished that) (Ogburn and Nimkoff 1955). In the process the family become more specialized, responsible mainly for regulating intimacy and caring for and socializing young children. Specialization has also been the name of the game in education as well, resulting not only in the differentiation of primary, secondary, and tertiary forms but also in the proliferation of many types of different-purpose institutions, such as community colleges, vocational schools, four-year colleges vocational schools, and research universities. Some European and other systems have separated higher learning into universities and research academies.

Proliferation: Adding New Functions to Existing Structures

Expanding business firms add new departments or divisions to handle new functions (sales divisions for new regional markets, human relations departments, research-and-development divisions) as their operations expand. So do government bureaucracies. In higher education, an example is the creation of multiple curricula in community colleges to accommodate academic programs necessary for transfer to four-year institutions, terminal vocational degrees, and "preparation for life" courses (Brint and Karabel 1989). We will also discover that proliferation has been a favored strategy for universities as well, adding one function after another, with a peculiar twist. The obverse of proliferation is the shedding of functions, either outright or through downsizing or outsourcing.

Coordination: Dealing with the Consequences of Increased Scale and Structural Change

The impact of all the above structural processes, considered together, is to produce not only larger but also more complex structures with many more moving parts. We owe it to Durkheim ([1893] 1997) who insisted that increases in social complexity (division of labor) inevitably occasion the need for new kinds of integration in society. That principle has been discovered and rediscovered in organizational studies, politics and administration, and in studies of whole societies (see Simon 2001), to say nothing of the administration of campuses and the coordination of multicampus systems. Coordination encompasses new demands for routine management, for ensuring that the many hands of complex organizations know what the others are doing, and for anticipating, containing, and handling conflicts among differentiated units and groups. This final principle constitutes an important modification of any simple theory of economies of scale, because increases in scale of all types demand new structures, mechanisms, knowledge, and accompanying financial resources to deal with size and complexity.

I submit this classification of structural changes—increase in unit size, segmentation, differentiation, proliferation, and coordination—*both* as a set of tools for analyzing the kinds of changes experienced by higher education *and* as a key to understanding phenomena in those institutions that may be otherwise baffling. Two points will emerge: (a) the "choice" of directions of structural change is constrained by external restrictions and opportunities, and (b) the different kinds of social change ramify in different directions, and express themselves in distinctive anomalies and contradictions, status hierarchies, strategic adaptations, and patterns of competition and conflict. We simply cannot unravel these ramifications without understanding institutions' structural situations.

A PECULIAR CASE IN HIGHER EDUCATION: STRUCTURAL ACCRETION

As the illustrations in the last section reveal, the history of higher education has revealed all the forms of structural change associated with growth. I would like to spend some time on a special form that involves growth, specialization, and proliferation, and applies mainly but not exclusively to universities. In search for a descriptive term, I have settled on the concept of "structural accretion," a composite form of growth.* Its simple definition is incorporation of new functions over time without, however, shedding existing ones (deletion) or splitting into separate organizations. It is a complex process reflecting, in the main, the following driving forces:

- Expanding as a result of new opportunities for activities, usually but not always relevant to the main missions of the university. Rosenzweig put the culture of growth simply: "The institutional impulse is not to restrain growth but to support it . . . Standing still . . . is contrary to the nature of the beast, and contraction is simply an abomination" (1998: 156).

- The fact that most growth has been a matter of mutual opportunism— the belief on the part of external agencies that universities are an appropriate or effective place to invest resources in line with their own interests and purposes, and the dependence of universities mainly on external subsidization.

- The power of academic competition and emulation in a highly stratified prestige hierarchy of institutions. Stadtman enunciated this as a principle: "the tendency for institutions to emulate the most prestigious, largest, and most secure colleges and universities" (1980: 95).

---

*The exact naming of this type of change itself has had a little history. In thinking about the phenomenon over the years, I had settled on the term "blistering" as connoting a growth on the side of an organism without disturbing its fundamental organic unity. (I had also conceived the idea of an "onion" principle, but my colleague Mac Laetsch, a botanist at the University of California, Berkeley, corrected this analogy and saved me embarrassment by reminding me that onions do not layer on the outside but grow by adding at the center; that reminder more or less shot down "onionization" as a principle.) A few months ago, at a meeting of a small administrator-faculty group on the Berkeley campus—called the Wellman group—several of my colleagues objected to "blistering" because of its negative connotations: blisters are painful and caused by irritation. Also, blisters go away on their own, unlike academic additions. I agreed that I did not want those connotations. My colleagues suggested "grafting" (which does not really seem to connote structural change), "bureaucratic creep" (also negative in its connotations and does not include all the kinds of changes I had in mind), and even "adventitious budding," an analogy from plant life (but difficult to explain). Karl Pister, a member of the group, suggested simply "accretion," which is a neutral word and does not carry the unwanted connotations. I accepted that term and am grateful to Karl; I added "structural" to give it more specific reference to the kinds of organizational change I have in mind.

- Organizational inertia, university politics, and the shortage of mechanisms to ensure the shedding of adopted activities.

The ingredients of accretion have been noted by observers of higher education. The accumulation of functions was captured fifty years ago by Clark Kerr's (1963) invention of the term "multiversity," connoting that accumulation. He also identified the inertial side by noting cryptically that "[c]hange comes through spawning the new than reforming the old" (Kerr 1963: 102). More recently Altbach observed that "[w]hen faced with new situations, the traditional institutions either adjust by adding functions without changing their basic character or create new divisions or institutes" (2001: 30). Diffusion through competitive copycatting has also been noted as a principle; "[institutions] build prestige by mimicking institutions that already have prestige" (Brewer, Gates, and Goldman 2002: 66). And faculty conservatism has been frequently identified as one of the most powerful forces in the academy (Kerr 1963); one critic speaks of "four hundred years of resistance to change in modes of instruction" (Marcus 2011: 41). Antagonism to change is a perhaps the most well-worn theme in academic humor. (Riddle: "What is more difficult to change than the course of history?" Answer: "A history course." Riddle: "How many Oxford dons does it take to change a light bulb?" Answer: "Change?"). Over the years, moreover, faculties appear to have cultivated the art of resistance commensurate with their levels of intelligence and ingenuity. After a long season of entrepreneurial efforts of running his proposal to establish the Said Business School through faculty committees at Oxford, John Kay concluded that the committee system had elevated the avoidance of decision making into a high art form. He identified "eight oars of indecision": deferral, referral, procedural objection, "the wider picture," evasion, ambiguity, precedent, and denial (Kay 2000). Perhaps he could have discovered even more than eight had he not been constrained by the metaphor of the rowing shell.

Despite these observations, I know of no general statement that integrates *all* these ingredients, much less traces out the ramifications of the process into almost every aspect of university life. I undertake both those tasks in these lectures.

A Historical Sketch of the Process

Here is a very brief, idealized history of the cumulative accretion in universities:

- In the colonial period and through the early nineteenth century, institutions taught and trained elite classes through the baccalaureate degree or its equivalents.

- Dramatized by Yale's introduction of the Ph.D. in 1860, universities consolidated postgraduate training during the last half of the nineteenth century, without, however, surrendering undergraduate studies.

- Also in the same period, professional schools of law and medicine were introduced as adjuncts to universities (Kimball 2009), and the list of professions served increased over time to include the long list with which we are now familiar. With respect to schools of education, universities came to supplement the work of the normal schools and teachers' colleges. This contrasted with the continued vitality of professional apprenticeship systems *outside* the universities in many other countries. Addition of professional education, however, did not result in the desertion of existing activities. They added to them and extended and intensified the "service to society and community" functions.

- Concomitant with the growth of postgraduate education, universities aggressively introduced and gave high priority and prestige to Humboldt's visions of research and created the academic department as the long-standing organizational venue for its execution. Over time, the number of departments has increased (e.g., the addition of the social sciences in the very late nineteenth century, and the addition of computer studies and communication studies in recent decades). So fundamental were these additions that by 1905 Abraham Flexner could declare that "the university has sacrificed the college at the altar of research" (quoted in Scarlett 2004: 39).

  More was to come. The philanthropic efforts of foundations such as the Rockefeller Foundation, as well as the federal government in the Vannevar Bush and post-Sputnik eras, expanded scientific research in universities to unprecedented heights. This spilled over in lesser degree to the social sciences and more negligibly into the humanities. As structural manifestations of expansion, we find campuses honeycombed with centers and institutes—called organized research units—that are often interdisciplinary and structurally separated from academic departments. Reflecting the increased role of government, many institutions of higher education developed "government relations" offices to keep contact and lobby with relevant agencies (McMillen 2010). Yet we also kept and expanded undergraduate, graduate, and professional education.

- The most recent phase (over the past thirty years) has seen the growth of sponsored and collaborative research with business organizations, sponsored research, collaborative research, and spin-off enterprises with faculty leadership. This also fits the pattern of accretion, and later we will treat the topic more fully, along with other "invasions" of commercial forces into campuses.

- Over time colleges and universities have expanded into international education, beginning with standard "junior year abroad" programs but recently becoming more diversified and extended into post-graduate and research activities—all part of the rapid globalization of higher education.

- As adjuncts to the standard baccalaureate programs, colleges and universities extended into the areas of correspondence courses, summer schools, workshops, and so on, to serve regular students who wanted to accelerate their progress or repeat flunked courses, professionals to improve their certification, and more mature students generally. Most colleges and universities tried to make these programs self-financing; they were also an important wedge for the practice of hiring temporary and part-time faculty.

- The most recent line of accretion in this family (along with the differentiation of private teaching institutions separate from the residentially based institution) is "distance learning," a huge and ill-understood series of changes, which Gregorian and Martin identified as the most important trend in higher education (2004). We only note this in the context of "accretion" at the moment and consider it separately later.

- From time to time universities have embedded more traditional "intimate" collegiate programs into their larger, department-dominated programs of "majors." I have in mind the Monteith College at the University of Michigan, and the Tussman and Muscatine experiments on the Berkeley campus in the 1960s and 1970s, as well as many less conspicuous interdisciplinary programs. Historically, these enterprises have proved to be vulnerable, largely because, unlike departments and other units, they are typically financed on a year-by-year basis and subject to discontinuation, and they rely on faculty who make requests for reduction of departmental teaching commitments in order to participate—requests that are not welcomed by department chairs.

- Over time colleges and universities added public entertainment (mainly in the form of intercollegiate athletic contests) and cultural enlightenment (museums, public lectures, dramatic and musical performances). Intercollegiate athletics is regarded by many as a cancer rather than an accretion, out of control because of pressures from alumni, media, and public love of competitive sports (below, pp. 93–94). With these also came intramural athletics and departments and programs of physical education, which, while often drawing faculty ridicule for having no place in academic institutions, persisted and grew all the same. These ancillary activities were also added to the institutions' other ongoing activities.

- Universities added academic presses as an avenue both for faculty publication of scholarly research (increasingly salient for tenure-track faculty members requiring evidence of such research as the most important ingredient for their professional advancement) and as a further instrument for cultural enlightenment of the public.

- Offices for Institutional Research have become common installations, providing the databases and analyses for the multiplicity of functions and complexity of decision making in complex organizations (Swing 2009) as well as public relations activities.

- Typically, universities and some colleges fashion accretions that are designed to create, consolidate, or produce *other* accretions. I have in mind fund-raising and development offices, campaign committees, alumni-relations offices, sponsored research offices, and technology-transfer offices. I could only experience a sense of irony when I came across a number of "advisory points" in a handbook on fund-raising for presidents: Appoint an extraordinary vice president for development with "an impressive office near yours" and membership on your top advisory council. Appoint a fund-raising consultant. Also, start a personal fund-raising library, conduct a feasibility study, and develop a case statement. Finally, "approve a budgetary allocation that is more than you are initially inclined to grant" [!] (Fisher 1994: 16).

- Social movements and other public pressures have added irregularly to the accretion process. The most notable examples are the spread

of academic programs and departments of women's studies, ethnic
studies, and gay and lesbian studies in the wake of external and
internal pressures associated with corresponding social movements.
Also opposed by some faculty for not having a proper academic
basis, these have nevertheless become standard features on many
university and college campuses. Combined internal and external
forces have most recently produced a growth of programs and departments in environmental studies.

- Among the great paradoxes of administrative accretion is that all
kinds of fortunes—both good and bad—provide motives for increasing it. In good times the motives seem self-evident. They call for
increases in administrative staffs for newly forming research institutes; augmentation of counseling; financial aid and other student
services; establishing and expanding sponsored research offices to
capitalize on expanding opportunities; and beefing up development
and fund-raising staffs to exploit expanding opportunities. Bad
times would seem to call for shrinkage of administration, but it does
not shrink. In the "new depression" (Cheit 1971) of the 1970s and
1980s, which involved shrinking enrollments and shrinking sources
of support, the rate of growth of administrative personnel between
the decade from 1975 and 1985 was 60 percent, while the growth
of faculty was only 6 percent (Zemsky, Wegner, and Massey 2005).
Why should a period of relative poverty call for such expansion?
The main causes are increased pressures to gain a competitive edge
in seeking students, securing financial aid, private gifts, and state
support—all diminishing but, *as a result*, calling for greater investment in staff simultaneously to squeeze out what can be squeezed
under the circumstances. Administering organizational cuts also
calls for staff time in determining what these might be and how
to deal with resistances to them. As a result of this paradox, there
seems to be no time in the history of colleges and universities that
does not call for some kinds of new administrative staff, whether to
maximize gains or minimize losses.

Such are the major lines of structural accretions that have in the long run
created the multiversity, or the distinctive American "bundle" referred to
by Parsons (1973). The process has been realized mainly in the universities, largely because they are less constrained by law and tradition from
expanding, and because external sponsoring agencies choose universities on account of their relatively unconstrained ability to take on new

activities and because they are, by knowledge and reputation, "the best." Donors, foundations, governments, and businesses prefer to choose "the best" to maximize the success of their own funding.

The accretion principle has also affected other segments of higher education, though less so than the universities, by mechanisms, as follows.

State colleges, many of them having evolved from teachers' colleges, have had a long history of competition with and emulation of the state's universities. This has taken the form of changing their names to "state universities"; striving for equity in teaching loads, salaries, and sabbatical relief; building research into their programs; and adding advanced degree programs (though most are excluded legally from offering the doctorate and some professional degrees). Many of these efforts involve adding programs and units, and thus constitute accretions. Status striving is the main engine: universities compete with one another for external sources as a means of expanding their activities, programs, and standing; state universities compete with universities to approach status equality. The long-standing striving of the polytechnics to gain parity with the universities in the United Kingdom is a conspicuous example from abroad.

Accretion in the community colleges is still another variant. As mainly public institutions they have traditionally been restricted to two-year degree programs (and prohibited from offering others), though some have succeeded in converting to four-year colleges, and many states now permit granting of baccalaureate degrees by community colleges—an accretion. Research at the community college level has been minimal. The main form of accretion has been curricular: continuing to offer preparatory liberal-arts transfer programs but expanding their curricula—typically in response to market opportunities and demands and the political influence of localities exercised directly and through governing boards—to offer more specialized vocational courses (Griffith and Connor 1994). The expansion of "preparation for life" courses without abandoning the other lines of instruction is a further example. Within each of three general categories, programs and units are added as demands or opportunities arise.

In addition to proliferation within organizations, the failure to abandon what has been added in the past is an essential ingredient of accretion. This is not a feature unique to educational institutions—organizational inertia is real and alive everywhere—but it is extreme in educational institutions, and it is important to understand why. I offer of the following considerations:

- There exists no ready mechanism for "going out of business" in the academy, as is possible through the mechanism of failure in commercial markets. Public institutions traditionally have been recipients of annually appropriated block grants from state governments as their main financial support, with varying degrees of control over specific programs or units within them. State governments are reluctant to let the institutions they have formed go out of business; it is difficult to imagine any one of the fifty states of the union deciding to junk one of "their" institutions—much less, the flagship university of the state—rational though that may be on administrative or economic grounds. Legislatures meddle in the administration of their institutions, but they are reluctant to kill them. Private institutions are governed more autonomously, though governing boards have also been reluctant to shut them down unless extreme economic conditions make it absolutely necessary.

- We must also point to the institution of academic tenure. Insofar as an academic unit involves tenured faculty as members, this constitutes a barrier to elimination. Tenure as an institution refers primarily to academic freedom, though over time it has accumulated the element of permanent job security. It is, in principle, legal and acceptable to terminate tenured faculty when units are eliminated (below, pp. 111–12). This occurs, but with great reluctance on the part of administrators, who either avoid the possibility or find places for tenured faculty in other units. The consequence is that "[tenure] inhibits managerial flexibility in moving faculty and changing academic institutions" (Rhoades 1998: 84). We will return to other aspects of academic tenure later.

- A third reason arises from a set of social science axioms that apply especially to academic institutions. The logic is as follows: if you take on a new *function*, you must add new a new *structure* to perform it (an organized research unit, an administrative division, a special office); if you create a structure you also create a *group* of people to staff it; and if you create a *group*, you also create a new *constituency*, one which, typically, includes as one its primary interests its own survival and enhancement. By this logic the process of proliferation of functions also generates internal political constituencies. These press their interests through strategies of argument, influence, and stonewalling, mainly in budget-preparing and budget-renewing seasons. It is a final part of this axiomatic system that administrators, for reasons of political survival, tend not to go in for outright killing of units but to shave around the edges. In hard times you stop cutting the grass, but you don't cut the faculty. Summarizing the patterns of cuts in the 1980s and 1990s, with many periods of budgetary adversity, Altbach cites the reluctance to alter drastically programs or priorities and instead to make broad, general cuts:

> [S]upport staff were eliminated and maintenance was deferred. A hiring freeze was put into place, salaries were frozen, and part-time teachers replaced full-time faculty. Libraries were unable to buy books, and journal collections were cut. Yet only a handful of colleges or universities violated the tenure of senior faculty. Departments were seldom eliminated, even where enrollments were low. Administrators tried to "protect the faculty," even at the expense of rational planning or institutional development. A few of the weakest private colleges merged or closed. Virtually no public institutions were closed, even where campus closures or mergers would have been in the best interests of the statewide system. (2001: 34)

As an external advisor to Yale social sciences in the 1990s, I witnessed that university's effort to eliminate, selectively, several "problematic" academic departments evolve first into a significant faculty revolt and then into the disappearance, through resignation, of three top administrators instead of the removal of several academic departments (for a brief account, see Rosenzweig 1998). On the other hand, recent history records some successful efforts to eliminate degree programs and departments, engineered with great dexterity (e.g., Kirwan 2006).

In the literature on higher education we do come across some talk of "unbundling," but most suggestions deal with outsourcing or privatization of activities without perceived direct educational functions: campus food services, bookstores, operation of student health services, security services, and plant and utility infrastructures (Langenberg 1999). Duderstadt (2000) also mentions admissions, counseling, and certification as possibilities for unbundling. There is discussion and some activity in outsourcing subjects like introductory language instruction to community colleges and elsewhere—subjects already "outsourced" to some degree *within* institutions to temporary faculty and teaching assistants. The actual cost reductions realized by outsourcing are no doubt highly variable. More ambitious attempts to eliminate the lower division (freshman and sophomore years) of baccalaureate-granting colleges and universities have failed (for two efforts at Stanford, see Cuban 1999), partly because of sentimental attachment to the "four-year degree" as an institutional stamp, partly because of resistance of intercollegiate athletics and alumni, and, by now, also because of the fact that the lower division provides the major sources of "employment" for graduate student teaching assistants. In a word, the talk and activity of unbundling seems more to confirm the *strength* of the accretion-bundling complex than it does its *reversal*.

THE DISCIPLINE-BASED ACADEMIC DEPARTMENT: SO STRONG AND YET SO FRAIL

One part of the great transformation of American higher education from the Civil War to the first decades of the twentieth century was the increased specialization of knowledge, both within existing areas of inquiry and by the appearance of new areas. These specializations moved from more diffuse areas of inquiry into "disciplines," connoting the production of knowledge on the basis of "disciplined" exploration of the subject matter by using an explicit and selective set of analytic assumptions and principles. These intellectual domains differed in rigor and completeness, and still do.

Irregularly but inevitably, the *organizational* embodiment of disciplines in the United States became the academic *department*, a largely autonomous subunit of faculty members in a discipline. This distinctive creation—Alain Touraine, the French sociologist, called the department "the great American invention" ([1974] 1997: 33)—had its origins and its cousins in European systems of "faculties," but it evolved, with variations, as a more collegial and less authoritarian model than those cousins. The "chairman"—now "chair"—even in its strongest manifestations, never reached the dictatorial dimensions of the chief, single "professor" in the German and other systems.

Despite this looseness, the department accumulated power over time and became the principal institutional reality of universities and colleges. Its constant feature is a defined, annually renewed budget and career lines. Its responsibilities have fanned out. Departments are mainly responsible for collegiate and post-graduate *curricula* and who teaches them; most "majors" are named after disciplines and administered by departments. Future professionals receive their *training* in discipline-based departments. Their professional *names*—physicist, geneticist, anthropologist—derive from this training. They find *employment* in discipline-based departments, and if they have not been certified in department-based training programs, they are scarcely employable (who will hire a "natural scientist" or a "humanist" without further specification?). *Advances* in their careers (rank, tenure, pay increases) are initiated and largely controlled by departments, though this power is shared with the editors of journal and with publishers of books, as well research-granting agencies, whose decisions govern the main products on which academics are assessed (Bowen and Schwarz 2005). Together, the graduate training and employment systems form discrete *labor markets* for disciplines, more or less sealed off from other disciplinary markets. And not least, once established, academic departments are notoriously difficult to *eliminate,* as administrators have learned and know well; they are the quintessential accretions. The main budgetary victims in difficult, downsizing times are weaker experimental and interdisciplinary enterprises that lack the same structural and budgetary foundations. Departments can be squeezed but seldom strangled.

Other institutional arrangements more or less mirror this discipline/department core of colleges and universities. Most professional social scientists with the same disciplinary name are members of a national—and perhaps regional and international—association bearing the name of their disciplines: the American Political Science Association, for example. These associations act as status-protecting and status-enhancing groups and political lobbies. They hold annual meetings, which are simultaneously occasions for intellectual activity, recruitment, socializing, and ritual affirmation of identity and solidarity. Commercial and university publishers honor the disciplines by developing publication lists with disciplinary names—the psychology list, the history list, and so on. Governmental and foundation funders organize their giving in part by discipline-named programs and appoint program officers with disciplinary designations. Honorary and fellowship-awarding societies—such as the National Academy of Sciences, the American Philosophical Society, and the Guggenheim Foundation—organize their membership lists and categories of award giving along disciplinary lines.

Thus, discipline-based departments persist as the lifeblood and seat of vested interests in institutions of higher education. From a social-psychological point of view, the facts that professionals describe themselves by disciplinary label, find their homes, and carry out their roles in discipline-based departments and associations mean that part of their personal and collective identities will be couched in a disciplinary frame. Departments are the structural bases for what have been called academic tribes with distinctive cultures—in-groups that write to, for, and against one another and bear loves and hates for others (Becher 1989). In everyday life faculty members continuously remind themselves and others and are reminded by others that they have such an identity. The fact that this institutional and personal identity is so pervasive contributes to the idea that disciplines are reified and described as *things* in our discourse.

Despite all these sources of solidity, the discipline-based department presents a number of dilemmas and frailties that are not fully appreciated—largely, perhaps, because of the mentioned reification. I have noticed and reflected on these in my own career, and present them for your reflection:

- The department as a force for expansion. The budget of departments is determined by a process of annual request and justification for faculty and staff positions, office costs, and other expenditures. The chair presents (or is presented with) a budget and may enter into a process of negotiation and adjudication with the administration. Expenses are controlled in this manner, but chairs, backed by their colleagues, exercise systematic pressure to expand or not be cut. One argument typically employed is that unless the department "covers the field" in teaching and research, it not only fails in its intellectual mission but also is also a lesser force in the national competitive arena. Relevant evidence: (a) Chairs of history departments are forever arguing, with fervor, that it is fatal for their entire program if Iberian history (or some other area) isn't covered. Administrators are continuously bombarded with this logic. (b) Multidisciplinary departments feel less favored because they believe that, if they were distinct, they would fare better competitively and be in a better position to expand. Joint departments of sociology and anthropology live under this tension, even if latent. One source of the discontinuation of the famous Department of Social Relations at Harvard (1946–1970) was restlessness on the part of its psychologists, anthropologists, and sociologists, based on the feeling that if they existed as separate departments they could compete better for faculty and resources than in their three-in-one arrangement. (c) Those departments that choose the strategy of developing strength by concentrating in delimited areas—small group research or criminology, for example—are seen to hobble themselves by not being able to "cover the field" and offering first-class *general* graduate training. All these factors generate self-protective or expansionist tendencies.

- The weakness of the chair. Given the "foreignness" of European dictatorial models, given the democratic thread in American society, and given the academic culture of "company of equals," it was probably foreordained that the chair would be a comparatively powerless position. Though there are exceptions (e.g., chairs in medical schools), in general the chair is low on authority and high on persuasion, coddling, diplomacy, coordination, and conflict management (Gmelch and Miskin 1995). I served as chair of my department twice during my career, and from those assignments I emerged with a working definition: "A department chair is a person that spends 80 percent of his or her time running errands on behalf of disagreeable colleagues." In retrospect I was wrong: 50 percent would be better, with 25 percent in dealing with factions and 25 percent in paperwork. Chairs carried much of the responsibility with respect to all aspects of affirmative action and subsequent diversification efforts. When I was chair I attended the annual meetings of sociology departmental chairs around the country; these gatherings tended to turn into group therapy sessions. I should add that departments with opportunities for external research funding experience an increase in individual faculty entrepreneurship and a decrease in collective faculty involvement in departmental life. Furthermore, the chair must continually negotiate with those researchers about teaching time to be bought off and deal with the chronic headaches of maintaining the department's teaching commitments.

While historically necessary and perhaps the best of worlds on balance, the chairmanship presents problems of weakness and tedium for incumbents and problems of motivation for potential incumbents. Many faculty regard it as an onerous distraction from more important work (mainly research), with the result that some of the most active and outstanding researchers make a career of avoiding the office. Correspondingly, some deans make a career of beating the bushes for willing and able people—and those not offensive to their colleagues—to take on the job.

- Structure and culture of departments. It is in the nature of scientific and scholarly activity to fragment and spread over time as new discoveries are made, new lines and subtraditions of research develop, and new uses for knowledge become evident. New interdisciplinary initiatives flourish and hybrid fields are formed. Sometimes these are significant enough that they become the basis of additional structures—research programs, even departments such as astrophysics and neuroscience, or multidisciplinary organized research units. Sometimes bypassed fields, such as zoology or geography, partially disappear and are reabsorbed into other units.

Despite these organizational adjustments, I must point to the fundamental structural rigidity of departments. This persists in the natural sciences even with the flexibility I just noted. In the social sciences and the humanities the rigidity is striking, with almost no change in disciplinary-departmental designation since they were introduced into higher education in the late nineteenth century. Yet all these fields show a continuing *intellectual* process of extension, diversification, and fragmentation. This means that the new directions are absorbed under one departmental roof. The consequences are paradigmatic incoherence in disciplines, more specialization, less comprehension of the whole discipline by its own members, and more internal conflict over priorities in faculty appointments and teaching responsibilities. Even in economics, which boasts greater paradigmatic unity than its sister social sciences, recent history has seen innumerable new subfields and preoccupations—development economics, agency theory, new institutional economics, and above all behavioral economics. All these are absorbed as subthemes in economics departments, and some become subsections in the professional associations. The appearance of new schools of thought and new intellectual emphases are forever pushing to extend the process. And while the long-standing subfields may undergo change, they seldom disappear altogether. All this is good news in that it reflects intellectual dynamism, but it creates problems of integration and synthesis of knowledge.

I have referred to these dynamics as a *contradiction* between the rigidities of structure (the department) and the dynamics of culture (the discipline), which yields a picture of departmental overloading, competition and conflict over priorities, and disciplinary sprawl. This contradiction is a running sore that is continuously dealt with but seldom formally acknowledged.

The Organized Research Unit as Distraction from Departments

Laurence Veysey (1965: 338) noted that the basic structure of the modern university was set in the early twentieth century with the consolidation of the research impulse and the academic department. The only subsequent structural innovation, he noted in a side comment, was the system of research centers or institutions, and these were expressions of the augmented research impulse.

An organized research unit is a university structure separate from an academic department. It is usually established as a response to an interest on the part of an external agency (foundation or government), which offers resources for some line of research to be launched and carried out. A recent instance is the creation of a number of research institutes on the study of different facets of terrorism, sponsored and financed by the Department of Homeland Security. Institutes and centers have a faculty director and an assemblage of affiliated faculty members (usually interdisciplinary), a physical location on or near the campus, and a supporting infrastructure. These units also have developed a staying power almost as strong as departments. Their director and affiliates are constituencies, believe in and proclaim the legitimacy of their efforts, and resist efforts to discontinue them. In a word, they, too, are accretions.

From the perspective of the academic department, the many research units on campuses provide alternate homes and foci of identification for its members. Typically, though not always, their research grants are administered through organized research units; this includes recruiting and hiring research assistants. These units also often provide clerical and staff support that is more generous than that available in departments. Since they are more intellectually focused than departments, the faculty member may find that his or her interests mesh more comfortably with others in research units than they do with departmental colleagues. Research units are also the setting for working groups, seminars, colloquia, and conferences, though they do not offer formal courses. All this adds up to the fact that, in addition to being intellectual supplements to departments, research units are also *competitors* with departments for loci of research, time spent, and intellectual commitment. Aware of this, I once described the academic department as an emptying residual, a place where the chair negotiates over what and how much faculty teach, and an arena in which colleagues fight over who gets hired and who does not. Perhaps it is not too much to say that departments have been hollowed out as intellectual communities but retain vitality as political entities. These are oversimplifications at best, but they take note of the fact that academic departments and organized research units are in some respects at cross-purposes in the knowledge arena—a point whose extent and significance are not fully appreciated.

REACTIONS AND CONFLICTS ENDEMIC IN THE PROCESS OF ACCRETION

Numerous commentators have noted a paradox of extremes in American higher education. It experiences simultaneous love and hate. It is asserted to be the best in world but at the same time is assaulted on multiple fronts. Altbach observed that "at the same time that American academe has come in for unprecedented criticism at home, it is widely emulated abroad" (2001: 11). During the 1990s I served on an international body called the German-American Academic Council, composed of about two dozen scholars, civil servants, and political leaders from both countries. A consistent theme was that the German members could find much to praise about the American system (especially its political decentralization and competition among universities) and almost nothing to praise about their own. In the meantime, the American members appeared to be noncommittal about the German system but quick to criticize their own on many counts. This anomaly produced a number of dialogues between the deaf.

I would like to develop this anomaly—this theme of ambivalence— further. In doing so, I will first enunciate a little model that has served me well as a scholar of social change. It goes as follows.

Social change typically has both destructive and constructive aspects. Schumpeter's (1934) notion of "creative destruction" captures the process. Industrial technology and its reorganization of the division of labor eliminated less efficient forms of production and introduced new ones. Computers replaced typewriters; cell phones crowd out landlines. The rise of democracy partially erased earlier forms of political life and established new principles of authority and political participation. Secularization eroded traditional religious cultures and ushered in new legitimizing cultural ideologies. This principle, while general, is usually not an all-or-none matter. Residues of past cultures and structures survive, and in some cases changes involve accretions—superimposing new arrangements on old ones. In all events, it seems inevitable from this double aspect that circumstantial change is greeted with ambivalence— both welcomed and resented. In addition, the human mind is sufficiently agile—or unruly, if you will—that one consequence of circumstantial change is that those affected by it select one side of this double aspect, generalize and extrapolate from it, and create runaway scenarios that result in predictions of both positive utopias (Pangloss) or negative ones (Cassandra).

To choose some general examples: film, radio, telephone, and television were hailed by some as world-shaking revolutions that would create a whole new world of efficiency in communication. Thomas Edison said in 1913 that with the invention of film "our school system will be completely changed in the next ten years" (quoted in Stokes 2011: 201). Others bemoaned their destruction of interpersonal intimacy and the end of confidentiality. Neither consequence was realized. The advent of radio and television brought predictions of the end of attendance at athletic events, and television promised the end of attendance at the movies. Early reactions to the computer crystallized into idealized views of the magic of the information society and predictions about the disappearance of meaningful social life (Streeter 2004). The e-mail and the Web have been proclaimed as both liberating and addictive. To choose more cosmic examples: Malthusian predictions of starvation and disaster accompanied the rosy glow of the idea of progress during the Industrial Revolution; Marxian predictions combined both a negative utopia (the excesses of capitalism) and a positive one (the perfection of communism) into one ideology. The darkness of environmental predictions of spoliation, destruction, and exhaustion are countered by scientific and economic arguments that new technologies will overcome the negative effects of old technologies. The lesson to be learned is that humans' assessments of their own histories and situations include not only realism but also galloping extensions of absolutes to create imaginary worlds of both utopian bliss and Chicken Little disaster. This lesson should impart a note of caution if not distrust in those extreme predictions.

The social sciences themselves reveal a long history of the Panglossian-Cassandrian syndrome. Anyone familiar with the literatures of industrial and economic development, urbanization, and community life will find these dual tendencies—the one extreme basking in the effects of prosperity, urbanity, and human betterment, the other bemoaning the impoverishment, depersonalization, and injustices. Sensible scholars of these phenomena find mixtures of all those effects in complex patterns of change.

I submit that the history of higher education—perhaps education in general—has been especially productive of the Panglossian-Cassandrian syndrome. Clark Kerr made a partial reference to this phenomenon when he observed, from his own experience at celebratory occasions, "What I have come to experience are references to a glorious past and to a fearsome future" (Kerr 1963: 211). His remark caught a part of my analysis. What I want to do is to give a more complex account and to argue that it is inextricably mixed with the phenomenon of accretion I am stressing. Let me produce a few historical illustrations:

- The nineteenth century, especially its last third, marked what is agreed to be perhaps the greatest transition in American higher education—a drift from an emphasis on received religious truths to the search for knowledge in general; a steady conquest of scientific emphases over religious ones; the incorporation of sciences into curricula; the Humboldtian view of research and the consolidation of specialized knowledge; and postgraduate degrees and professional schools. All these meant the death knell for the early nineteenth-century college. As Ruben (1996) has documented, however, the whole process was accompanied by punctuated counterstatements: periodic, nostalgic reassertions of the sacred value of religious and moral education. Then, at the beginning of the twentieth century, a full-fledged countermovement developed. Here is how she summarizes the situation:

  > By the end of the first decade of the twentieth century criticism of higher education had become so commonplace, one educator quipped, that "nobody has a good word to say for the college." After decades of belittling the old-style college, a new note of nostalgia entered public discourse about higher education. Commentators [e.g., Nicholas Murray Butler] missed the unity, moral purpose and high ideals of the classical college. They perceived the new universities as chaotic and materialistic, and their students as selfish and undisciplined. This criticism escalated over the next decade, growing as universities' various efforts to keep knowledge and morality united in a modern form of moral education failed. (Ruben 1996: 230; see also Veysey 1965)

  All the ingredients of my "model" of transitional conflict are there: dismissal of an archaic past *and* glorification of a brave new world by the riders of the crest of change, as well as glorification of a treasured past *and* dread of ruination by the apparently conquering wave of change. In fully developed form, such conflicts involve the evocation of four utopias, two positive and two negative, two past and two future, arrayed in juxtaposition to one another. These utopias differ, of course, as to how explicit and how fully developed they are.

- I interpret the wave of antivocationalism of the first third of the twentieth century—voiced most forcefully by the powerful voices of Thorstein Veblen and Robert Hutchins—and the ideal systems of truth seeking that promised to save a vanishing world as a manifestation of the Pangloss-Cassandra principle. In 1909 John Chapman moaned that "[the] men who control [universities] are very little else than businessmen" (quoted in Aronowitz 2000: 17). Hutchins claimed that "[the pursuit of knowledge for its own place is being rapidly obscured [by vocationalism] in universities and may soon be extinguished" (1936: 36). Veblen announced simply that a college of commerce is "incompatible with the collective cultural purpose of the university." "It belongs," he said, "in the corporation of learning no more than a department of athletics" ([1918] 1968: 154). The antivocational theme has continued noisily up to the present (e.g., see Aronowitz 2000, whose subtitle reveals both a negative and a positive utopia: "Dismantling the Corporate University and Creating True Higher Learning").

- Immediately after World War II, as Congress was moving toward the historic passage of the GI bill, some opposing voices of college administrators to this almost-universally approved measure were heard, complaining that the flood of these "nontraditional" students would constitute a threat to the values of isolation and pastoral bliss of their idealized campuses (Thelin 2004a: 263).

- I will note later the opposition to the innovations that were being pressed with the support of philanthropic foundations earlier in the twentieth century, mainly on the theme that these foundations—expressing corporate values—were going to supplant the traditional values of academe in corporate directions.

- The long-term march of and conquest of research among the rewarded activities of university life has created periodic periods of protest and proclamations that liberal education in particular and undergraduate education in general have been denuded or destroyed. At the height of the federal bonanza of research support by the federal government in the 1960s, Nisbet (1971) complained of its degradation and corruption of academic values. The very influential manifesto by Boyer (1990) in the wake of a flood of bashing colleges and universities for their educational failures in the 1980s (Bennett 1984; National Institute of Education 1984; Association of American Colleges 1985) is perhaps the most notable protest against the consequence of the research emphasis. A more recent critic has declared a "great ripoff" by universities, proclaiming that "[t]he research emphasis versus the teaching emphasis is at the heart of the deterioration of undergraduate education in America" (Scarlett 2004: 39; see also Tussman 1997). There is some truth in these declarations, but at the moment I point only to the their absolute and unqualified features.

- The rise of online instruction shows a similar bifurcation of reactions. On the one hand, we learn that "DIY [Do It Yourself] education promises [an] evolution from expensive institutions to expansive networks"and "aims to fulfill the promise of universal education, but only by leaving the university behind" (Kamanetz 2010: 119). Another enthusiast asserts that the "disruptive innovation" of computer learning "will change the way the world learns" (Christensen, Horn, and Johnson 2011). It is "destroying the traditional classroom and replacing it with an even better way to learn and teach" (William Draves, quoted in Stokes 2011: 197). At the same time, we notice a widespread feeling among academics—a feeling combining denial and dread—that online education is a denigration if not a corruption of traditional modes of education; "[the] new technology of education . . . robs faculty of their knowledge and skills, their control over their working lives, the product of their labor, and ultimately, their means of livelihood" (David Noble, quoted in Stokes 2011: 198).

- In keeping with larger trends, the 1980s saw an upsurge of an "accountability mania" in industry and in federal and state governments—more on this in the chapter 3. This also spread to academia. One of its ingredients was to develop "performance indicators" such as test scores of graduating students, graduation rates, and job placement. Reactions to this also bifurcated. An Australian team of academic administrators noted in 1998 that "[s]omething resembling a . . . cult seems to have grown up around the notion of performance indicators, so that all manner of powers and virtues are ascribed to them and expectations are aroused by citing their great benefits and miraculous results" (quoted in Gaither, Nedwek, and Neal 1994: 13). In the meantime, administrators and faculty were assaulting these and other measures of performance not only as methodologically flawed when applied to academic institutions but as fatal threats to academic autonomy, institutional trust, and even academic freedom (below, pp. 85–89).

More generally, some authors have commented on "management fads" that rise and fade in academia as elsewhere—zero-based budgeting,

benchmarking, total quality management, and business process reengineering. These innovations reveal common features: a narrative and
rhetoric of their own, with magical problem-solving or revolutionary
potential (Birnbaum 2000). The ideas are diffused and disseminated in a
definite pattern, which is inevitably temporary. Insofar as these innovations are accompanied by assertions that a crisis is at hand and a cure is
in sight, they are simultaneously Cassandrian and Panglossian.

Conditions Producing the Endemic Pattern

To conclude the current discussion, I mention four factors—
simultaneously causal and reinforcing—of this Panglossian-Cassandrian
process that accompanies changes in the structure of higher education:

- Earlier I mentioned the distinctive moral embeddedness of higher
  education. That context provides a special type of cognitive-
  evaluative frame, encouraging the tendency to define issues in
  extreme, totalistic, and good-and-evil terms. The prospect of the disappearance of the old is regarded alternatively as good riddance or
  tragic loss; the arrival of the new is regarded alternatively as defile-
  ment or new-world-creating. Moreover, the moral mental set is con-
  ducive to various types of one-factor, simplistic thinking and does
  not welcome contingent, conditional, and qualified assessments.

- I also mentioned the special strength of inertial tendencies among
  academics, and their highly honed capacity—both psychological and
  organizational—to block changes in valued aspects of their way of
  life. One of the most effective strategies of resistance is to escalate
  them to an expression of high-minded principle ("the barbarians
  at the gates"), which is consistent with both the moralistic and the
  arrogant tendencies of much of academic culture. This strategy also
  produces extreme statements.

- Closely related, we should note the considerable rhetoric power that
  lies in the language of alarm, crisis, and salvation. In particular, the
  language of crisis is typically not only a description of a state of affairs but also a "dramaturgic term, suggesting urgent problems that
  require immediate heroic solutions" (Donaghue 2008: 1). As such, it
  is a mobilizing device. "The rhetoric of crisis does not seek to further
  analysis, but to promote action and advance the priority of an issue

on the always-overcrowded public policy agenda" (Birnbaum and Sushok 2001: 70). It aims to accomplish this purpose by developing a history and narrative that highlights the exceptional, the threatening, and the urgent. It is of additional persuasive value to generalize the rhetoric and to claim that the crisis is fundamental and moral, not merely technical or practical. Because the language of crisis is overused historically, because so many proclaimed crises turn out not to be crises, and because the language of crisis becomes deflated as a result, a further rhetorical device emerges: to claim that the crisis at hand is a "real crisis," acknowledging tacitly the unreality of past ones.

- The language of crisis and evocation of extremes rests, finally, on the presence of a pervasive mythology among many academics: nostalgia for an imagined past reality of the university as a happy mix of the principles of collegiality, common commitment to a calling, and a company of equals. I sometimes experience those feelings myself.

I will return to this theme of ambivalence in the final chapter when I assess special topics such as part-time academic employment, commercialization, and for-profit enterprises. To telegraph that discussion, I will attempt to move away from the pattern of extremes of ambivalence and produce more textured and complex accounts that are perhaps less intellectually and emotionally satisfying but more in keeping with current realities.

TWO LONG-TERM CONSEQUENCES OF ACCRETION

In this volume, I posit that many additional features of university life trace to and reflect the fundamental phenomenon of accretion. I close this chapter by mentioning two of the most obvious.

The Structuring of Faculty Activities

As functions and structures are accumulated, there are two primary consequences for faculty life:

- Personal workload increases and becomes more diversified. More activities are added when the academic becomes more than a teacher, evaluator of students, advisor, and role model. He or she is now called upon to conduct research of high quality; to manage a laboratory or a group of research assistants; to write letters of recommendation for students; to apply for grants; to file reports on research activity; to spend more time in evaluating research grant proposals for foundations and government funding agencies; to consult with community groups, foundations, and government; to attend conferences and congresses; and to spend more time in the air. (Jacques Barzun [1968] wrote of "academics in orbit," and we used to jest that Berkeley faculty conformed to the policy of the Strategic Air Command—one professor in the air at all times.) Surveys of university faculty consistently show that they work 50 to 60 or more hours per week. Many factors go into these figures—for example, that no amount of scientific and scholarly output is "enough" in the struggle for status and esteem—but I would attribute them mainly to the accretion and fragmentation of their work activities. The increasingly complex "bundle" created by accretion fosters a correspondingly complex "bundle" of university-related activities on the part of its individual faculty members. At least one handbook focuses on strategies for juggling faculty time and attention (Bianco-Mathis and Chalofsky 1999). Some researchers have attempted to demonstrate that role overload and role conflict are sources of psychological stress among academics (Fisher 1994).

I noticed this phenomenon directly when I was a visiting professor on the campus of Illinois State University (Bloomington-Normal) in the spring of 2006. For a number of years the institution had been sending messages to its faculty that research activities (mainly journal articles and research reports) were going to be given more attention in their advancement and promotion. Yet I also noticed (and commented in a brief article in a campus publication) that no corresponding reduction in teaching activities had been enacted or contemplated.

- With this increased pressure on faculty, the long-term tendencies to increase the size of student bodies on campuses, and the astronomical increase in funding that would be required to assign regular faculty to teach those numbers, several lines of *differentiation* of the faculty role have made their appearance. One line has been the growth of curriculum and career advisors in the administration, who gradually assume responsibility for one traditional activity (student advising) toward which faculty had become both indifferent and ineffective—but still formally responsible—over the years.

The addition of psychotherapy and counseling to student health services was a further transfer of faculties' responsibilities as moral authorities. More importantly, I refer to the expansion in numbers and responsibilities of teaching assistants (graduate lab and section leaders and exam evaluators), undergraduate "readers" of exams, part-time graduate and some undergraduate research assistants, nonfaculty research personnel (hired mainly through research institutes on "soft" grant monies), and appointments of both full-time and part-time lecturers and instructors (of which we will hear more later). All of these classes are ancillary to the tenure-track faculty and reflect the partial renunciation of traditional faculty responsibilities. Two features characterize these classes:

a. Ancillaries tend to increase during periods of rapid expansion. In the frantic days of growth of students and research opportunities in the period between 1950 and 1970, for example, their numbers exploded, while growth rates of "regular" faculty were very modest by comparison (Smelser 1974). Paradoxically, as we will see later, the very same classes, contingent faculty especially, also tend to expand in institutional hard times, but by a different dynamic— administrative economizing and achieving flexibility in curricular offerings.

b. While these groups were assigned to undertake some core *activities* of teaching and research, the faculties as established elites of the university were reluctant to relinquish *control* of them or to compromise the claim that the faculty remained the academic heart, soul, and conscience of their institutions. This was accomplished by several mechanisms. Approval of curricula and courses remained largely in control of designated faculty committees; faculty kept formal responsibility for evaluating students and signed and legitimized their grade sheets; the role of "principal investigator" in sponsored research was restricted to regular faculty members, thus limiting independent initiatives on the part of nonfaculty research personnel, except informally; nonfaculty research personnel could teach only on an incidental basis and with approval by faculty committees. All the ancillary categories were excluded from membership in academic senates and councils, shared governance, and symbolically important privileges such as parking. All this represents a classical example of elites' delegating responsibility but not power and privilege—incidentally, also, an important source of political alienation.

These processes expectably produced several classes of second-class citizens in the university community. Each class participates in the core functions of the institution but is denied the power, prestige, and honor of those who control those functions. Administrative advisers and consultants to students are consigned to that category of "staff," many of whom are convinced that they really run the university and whom many faculty members ignore when they do their job well and are quick to blame when they appear not to do so. Nonfaculty research personnel sometimes engage, usually unsuccessfully, for academic senate membership, faculty privileges, and formal teaching (Smelser 1974). (I once defined a university as an arena in which the faculty spend most of their time successfully avoiding teaching and nonfaculty researchers spend most of their time unsuccessfully agitating to teach.) A further expression of status dissatisfaction is that the most active arenas for faculty unionization in recent decades have been among contingent faculty members and teaching assistants, not regular faculty (below, pp. 109–10).

Implications for Academic Community

The changes of academic community occasioned by accretion are by now so evident that they require little demonstration. The main mechanisms have been these:

- The sheer size of the faculties of major universities. With 2,000 or more "colleagues," a professor can pass through a whole career on his or her own campus without meeting, much less getting to know, more than a small percentage of them. Large numbers also dictate corresponding increases in social distance and superficiality between faculty and administrators and faculty and students.

- Increased specialization and fragmentation. This has been accomplished through the growth in numbers and "silo-ization" of discipline-based departments with specialized languages and interests, as well as "internal silo-ization" of these departments as their subject matter specializes and sprawls.

- The addition of many ancillary, especially nonacademic, activities and programs. These activities have created diversity and tended to turn the university into an aggregate of programs and activities with little organic relationship to one another. Even early in the twentieth century, one commentator could speak of the campus as an aggregation of incompatibles—"a combination of sporting resort, beer garden, political convention, laboratory, and factory for research as confused as a Spanish omelet" (Canby 1936: 81; for a more recent version of the same observation, see Geiger 2004: 15). This aggravated enduring cleavages and conflicts over priorities, most notably the long-standing tension between academics and athletics as well as academics and partying.

- The creation of research-fund-seeking faculty entrepreneurs. Such entrepreneurism leads to individualizing and separating effects, as individual faculty members reach out externally to different sponsors of research.

- The domination of discipline-based research. This drives faculty identification toward professional associations and disciplinary brethren in other institutions and away from identification with home institutions. Lord Ashby spoke of a crisis of identity: "The modern academic suffers a divided loyalty between the university he serves and the professional guild (of chemists or historians and so on) to which he belongs." (1974: 73). Internationalization of disciplines only extends the problem, as do opportunities for rapid electronic communication outside the community and nation.

What university community remains is "a whole series of communities" (Kerr 1963: 1), and perhaps a residual general community that is largely imagined or supposed, one proclaimed on ceremonial occasions by campus leaders and governing boards, at athletic events, and in times of political crisis. If I may end this chapter on a personal, somewhat ironic note, I confess that I often feel that my university is a community, that I am a member of it, and that I love it as a community. Those feelings are genuine enough, but I do not, I think, take the next step and delude myself into a view that that community really exists.

TWO

The Dynamics Ramify

ACADEMIC POLITICS, CONFLICT, AND INEQUALITY

To summarize the first chapter, I laid out a number of types of change that have characterized American higher education—increase in unit size, segmentation of units, differentiation (or specialization and complexity), proliferation of functions, and coordination. I identified one principle of change that to me seems especially salient; it is observable at all levels, and dramatically so in the research university. I called it "structural accretion." The idea is simple enough. Growth is achieved by adding structures "on the side" of existing structures, but, critically, older structures are not shed in the process, even though their salience may change. The result is, over time, to create a kind of multifunctional monster with a diversity of structures, roles, and groups. My main aim was both to describe the accretion process and to trace a few of its many ramifications as a way of explaining what transpires in these institutions. I first analyzed the peculiarities of the quintessential accretion, the academic department, along with remarks about research centers, and institutes. Then I identified a particularly intensive and polarized kind of conflict that accompanies innovation and the production of new accretions. Finally, I turned, sequentially, to the relation of accretions to the overloading of faculty activities and the decline of academic communities.

What does all this add up to? One set of commentators recently described the modern elite research university as an "agile elephant" (Paradeise and Thoenig 2011: 10). This is very colorful, but upon reflection I have concluded that it is only half-true. The description applies best to institutions' and leaders' behavior during periods of growth, which must be "agile" in the face of competition for external support and funding for new enterprises (accretions), and the result of all the accretions has been to produce an elephantine creature. It may also apply to hard times when leaders scramble desperately for new lines of activity, even less profitable ones, in their need for resources. However, it does not characterize the second component—namely, the resistance to shedding. Here the qualifying adjective for the elephant becomes "reluctant" or "stubborn." Another way of putting this is that the dynamics of growth are different from the dynamics of shrinking (or, in this case, not shrinking). Growth involves seeking or accepting resources, taking advantage of opportunities, building new units, justifying the intended use of resources, bringing on new personnel, and incorporating them into the institution. Nonshrinking involves mechanisms of inertia, vested interests, in-fighting, and incremental and artistic pruning and shaving. Growing is thus more fun than shrinking, even though both processes involve a great deal of competition and conflict.

In this chapter, I push the implications developed in chapter 1 further. I analyze first the implications of institutional stability resulting from accretion, and how institutions respond to external instabilities. Then I turn to the growth of internal and external constituencies; the implications of this growth for group conflict, administration and academic politics; and, finally, the implications of accretion for systems of academic stratification and institutional prestige.

INSTABILITIES IMPOSED ON INERTIAL STABILITY

First, I take up a special range of dynamics. While accretion is one source of growth-related instability for institutions, it does not exhaust those sources. The *results* of accretion leave a residue of inertia—the stubborn elephant—that makes it difficult, in different ways, to respond to external instabilities. I classify these instabilities as (a) the python-and-goat principle (b) economic fluctuations, and (c) competitors for finite resources. I consider them in order.

Of Pythons and Goats

The python-goat imagery is a vivid way of describing the impact of certain demographic variations. The most dramatic example is the enormous leap in birth rates during the baby boom after World War II. That created a large population cohort (a goat) that had to be swallowed all at once. That cohort marched through the life cycle (the python) making demands for growth and adaptation and threatening to wreck, sequentially, one institution after another—pediatric care, primary schools, secondary schools, higher education, some job markets, therapy for midlife crises, then hospitals and retirement systems. It also echoed into subsequent boomlets of children as it reached reproductive age—and gave rise to talk of "tidal waves" of population derived from the original bulge. One peculiar feature of demographic goats is that their ingestion sometimes follows a period of starvation and is sometimes followed by another one; the birth rate of the 1950s and 1960s is again an example, following the small cohorts of he depression years, and experiencing the relative shrinkage afterward. The effect was a period of underdemand, followed by a massive growth, followed by a period of excess capacity and then slower growth if not stagnation in the 1970s.

Furthermore, the arrival of a goat creates other kinds of goats. The baby boomers created a boom for faculty in their time, as well as expansion of administrative offices dealing with housing, financial aid, advising, and student affairs—all accretions that increased costs and crystallized into visible constituencies. The faculty goat is especially interesting, because, with tenure, it did not shrink after a few years of its arrival and took decades to move through the system, constituting a source of ever-increasing costs with its advancement through the ranks, merit increases, and cost-of-living adjustments. Ultimately, this faculty goat generated a heightened concern with early retirement, phased retirement, and other schemes (especially salient, since the nation decided on an aggravating policy—uncapping the age limit—in the early 1990s). After very high rates of retirement did set in, attention turned to the problems of sapping retirement funds that did not anticipate the demands and which, in any event, were suffering from the increased longevity of their recipients and periodic battering of their equity bases in financial hard times.

Some "goats" are not demographic but originate in public policies. Such were the effects of the GI bill, preceding the baby-boom effect but introducing millions of returning veterans into institutions that had been emptied of male students during World War II. The federal legislation enacting the Pell Grants (student support based on need) in 1972 was not the result of a demographic bulge, but it meant an increase in the potential supply of students who could not otherwise afford college. The demands for affirmative action also constituted an abrupt change, beginning in the late 1960s and thereafter, in the *kinds* of students, staff, and faculty—based on race, ethnic group, and gender—expected to be admitted or hired. Furthermore, the realization of these goals through special admissions programs or open admissions raised issues of remediation and compensatory education, and occasioned widespread adaptive responses, such as the creation of equal opportunity programs and divisions, counseling offices, remedial programs (Bettinger and Long 2007), and special curricula (Sadovnik 1994)—all themselves accretions to meet the new challenges and with their administrative costs and inertial tendencies. Superimposed on such abrupt changes have been long-term ones, such as the growth of the population generally, the growth of groups of immigrants with their mix of expectations about education, and the steadily increasing demand on the part of "nontraditional" categories of students.

All these phenomena are on the demand side; they spill over, however, to the supply side. One example: In the heyday of the 1960s expansion, credentialed higher education faculty were in critically short supply. Furthermore, given the long time lag involved in producing advanced degrees, especially the doctorate, supply could not keep up, despite efforts of training institutions to respond. It was a heady seller's market, and colleges and universities began to hire pre-Ph.D.s and non-Ph.D.s at higher rates. Then, as the increased demand for Ph.D.s began to yield a larger supply of them, the baby-boom goat had passed through the collegiate years, demand was reduced, and around 1970 the academic market soured and turned abruptly to a buyer's market.

Economic Fluctuations

To introduce this topic is not to change the subject entirely but to add a set of instabilities beyond having to ingest, digest, and empty out goats of various sizes and descriptions. The continuity is that economic fluctuations—mainly periods of prosperity and periods of slowdown or recession—have a similar range of effects and set similar dynamics in process. Several general principles can be adduced:

- The dynamics of economic fluctuations are different for private institutions than for public institutions. Downward economic turns often reduce the size of endowments and the capacity and willingness of donors to donate. These effects also are felt by publics with private support, but the main mechanism for publics is that diminished economic activity affects state tax revenues, which translate into pressure to reduce state expenditures on higher education; state budgets are very responsive to economic changes (Zumeta 2004: 83–84). Beginning in the 1990s, an asymmetry set in: " [g]ood economic times brought less restoration and bad times brought greater deterioration" (Geiger 2004: 45). Fluctuations in federal research support affect both private and public institutions, mainly the elite ones. On balance, though there is enormous variation among types of fluctuations and among their effects, the privates seem generally better protected from them than the publics (Vest 2005). For example, with the great financial crash of 2008, equity holdings fell in value, usually in the 20–40% range, whereas the immediate impact on the publics—less dependent on equity markets—was less severe. As the crisis proceeded, however, the reduced revenues of state governments hit the publics very hard, and the privates gained some relief through the partial rebound of stock markets.

- Fluctuations resemble goats in that they create seasons of expansion followed by demands for retrenchment; they also trigger the same range of responses in years of plenty and years of hard times. Effects are particularly pronounced when post-goat years coincide with independent downward fluctuations in the economy. The most dramatic episode of such coincidence was in the early 1970s when the boom's babies had, by and large, passed through the system of higher education at the same time as the OPEC crisis struck, saddling the entire society, including its education system, with stagnation and inflation, declines in state revenues and federal research, spiraling costs, and subsequent taxpayer revolts (Stadtman 1980).

- Fluctuations produce a set of social-psychological reactions as well, though I confess that describing this effect is based more on my personal observations as a seasoned citizen of the university scene than on systematic data. The psychological effects of lean seasons associated with fluctuations are strong and real, and they tax all campus constituencies, which struggle with falling morale, gloom, hostility expressed toward parties thought to be to blame, and the bitterness of the conflicts that retrenchment fosters. At the same time, once things start to brighten again, rapid forgetting sets in and a sense of happy normalcy and academic-business-as-usual returns equally quickly. I remember this as the ravages of the early 1970s passed, as the trauma of the mid-1980s passed, as the early 1990s turned from retrenchment to the headiness of the late 1990s. The years from the dot-com collapse of 2002 and the financial crash of 2008 seem different, imposing a prolonged season of hardship, emergence from which is difficult to discern or predict. I will comment on this apparent "perfect storm" in chapter 3.

- I should also mention political conflicts experienced in higher education. Even though these are usually not cyclical in character and differ in their impact on institutions, they are frequently traumatic and generate serious consequences. I refer to conflicts such as the witch-hunting in the McCarthyism years, periodic waves of student activism, the antiwar and racial-ethnic-gender wars of the mid-1960s into the 1970s, the lesser but consequential protests for divestment from South Africa in the 1980s, and student protests over rises in tuition associated with repeated budgetary bludgeoning of public institutions in the past two decades. One might also mention the waste-inefficiency-lack-of-accountability onslaught on colleges and universities at both the state and federal levels, beginning in the

1980s, and the imposition of accountability measures that followed (below, pp. 85–87). These crises impose costs on colleges and universities in the form of crisis-management expenses (police expenses, for example, and machinery for meeting accountability requirements; Zdziarski et al. 2007). They also threaten to tax their good will and credibility of institutions and they increase administrators' and trustees' skittishness about public confidence, trust, and support for their institutions.

- One consequence of both economic jolts and political crises is that they tend to push the institution in a centralizing direction (Rourke and Brooks 1966). This is not an ironclad law, but the logic is as follows. Cost-income squeezes and episodes of conflict and public criticism create *systemic* problems for the institution and must be addressed from the center. Individual units are not inclined to self-adjust budgetarily; decisions about shifting, shaving, and cutting are general allocative problems for budgetary officers and other administrators. Many political crises also affect the integrity of the entire institution and call for coordinated and centralized action. Furthermore, when such crises affect multicampus systems—as in the case of annual budgetary hacking by state legislatures—allocative decision making moves toward the center, even though system-wide authorities may—and most often do—delegate implementation decisions to individual campuses (Burke 1999).

- Once decision making is mobilized at the center in response to crises, there is also a tendency for what I have called continued "centralization by default," whereby the center, having been mobilized for crisis management, continues to take an interest in the issue at hand and similar ones, and assumes a centralized monitoring role, often aimed in dealing with the fallout from previous crises, or to ready itself for similar ones that might arise. Administrative monitoring tends to remain in place if not actively challenged, and some campuses that have experienced political turbulences establish crisis-management machinery in anticipation of future ones.

Competitors for Resources

It is a truism that potential pools of support for institutions of higher education are constrained by the competing demands of other claimants at any given time. Annual state budgets express complicated compromises among demands from multiple groups. Federal research and scholarship commitments are expressions of what is available *in relation to* military, welfare, and other federal expenditures. And there are many claimants for private giving besides universities—community service organizations, museums, and hospitals.

These competitive demands fluctuate with the occurrence of foreign wars, with the condition of the economy, and with politicians' bids to groups considered salient in upcoming elections. In recent decades there has been a steady impingement on public funds available for public institutions, fostered by two forces: first, continuing political demands on the part of competing constituencies representing health, welfare, primary and secondary education, and correctional institutions (for some figures, see Cohen and Noll 1998: 49–50); and second, the tendency for competing demands to be established in the form of entitlements and quasi-entitlements, leaving higher education more vulnerable to annual budgetary fluctuations. Another factor that contributes to educational cutting is the (often only tacit) knowledge that higher education is one of the few public expenditure–supported institutions that can, by raising tuition and fees, more or less immediately recoup some if not all of their losses by generating income. Such alternatives are not available to correctional institutions, pension systems, and many health-care providers.

It is also true, however, that colleges and universities, despite attacks on them, continue to enjoy general reputations as successful, valuable, and prestigious institutions. They have argued forcefully that they are technological and economic assets for the growth of state and regional economies and for a nation struggling in an increasingly competitive global economy (Slaughter 1991). At the same time, higher education faces some permanent political disadvantages. Its numbers are small when compared to those of state civil servants, K–12 teachers, welfare recipients, and crime-apprehensive citizens. Higher education is therefore a comparatively weak political constituency. Furthermore, it suffers from the effects of economic and political short-termism. The effects of starving higher education are not immediately felt, even though the long-term deterioration of social, intellectual, and cultural capital may be devastating to states and the nation. By the time that the long-term effects of short-termism have taken their toll, moreover, it is a formidable task to reverse the process. It seems a general principle that, in political democracies with periodic elections, assertions of general prestige, respect, and long-term value cannot hold a strong candle in the struggle with immediate concerns of voters with electoral muscle. I regard this cultural, political, and economic mentality of short-termism to be perhaps the greatest threat of all to higher education in the coming decades.

In summary, the modern history of higher education is characterized by abrupt changes and cycles at all levels, and much of the turbulence of the market for students and the market for faculty and staff—and their relations to one another—can be written as a story of these irregularities. Gross fluctuations of these types are mainly significant for the system as a whole. Individual colleges and universities differ in their vulnerability. The elite research universities and highly selective four-year liberal arts institutions, which have large applicant pools in relation to numbers of students admitted and little difficulty in recruiting faculty, are less affected by swings. Middle-level institutions are moderately affected. The greatest pressures are felt at small, independent private and religious institutions that are less selective and have smaller endowments and are more dependent on student fees.

Relevance to Accretion

I conclude this section by relating this discussion of goats, economic instabilities, and competitive pressures to the principle of accretion. By virtue of that principle and the mechanisms associated with it, abrupt demands for growth are easier to deal with than periods calling for reducing excess capacity. Institutions like to grow, even though they face challenges in securing resources, assimilating new classes of citizens, building new structures, and facing opponents of change. As indicated, growth tends to involve less and less bitter conflict; decades ago Jencks and Riesman observed that "[it] is always easier to redistribute resources and power in periods of growth, because the progressives can be given more without the standpatters appearing to get less" (1968: 21). To shrink, however, calls for discontinuing units and sending people away, dealing with diminished campus morale, confronting vested interests, and jurisdictional fighting among those desperate not to be displaced. Decision makers fall out of favor and perhaps out of their offices because of political opposition. I remember a moment in the middle 1980s at the University of California— a period of serious lull in financial support for the institution—when President David Saxon issued a call to the academic senate to develop policies for dealing with "transfer, consolidation, discontinuation and disestablishment" of academic units. It was a reasonable proposal, considering the times. But it exploded like a bombshell; when officers of the senate were called upon to consider it, they fell into fighting over whether tenure was a system-wide or a campus matter and split on the issue of whether potentially displaced tenured faculty had claims on positions on other campuses. The senate never agreed on a shrinkage policy, even a hypothetical one, and as times began to brighten the issue was happily shelved without resolution. To put the matter bluntly: as a fallout from the principle of accretion, the agile elephant comes alive during abrupt demands for growth, and the stubborn elephant comes alive in periods of shock, responding to some degree under failing resources but doing so haltingly, minimally, and in the crossfire of angry constituencies.

ACCRETION AND THE GROWTH OF POLITICAL CONSTITUENCIES

Earlier I identified accretion as one source of institutional inertia. I now push the political implications of that process further. I divide the subject into internal and external constituencies—a division in many ways difficult to defend (Balderston 1974)—and then enunciate a few principles about how these constituencies impinge on academic life.

Internal Constituencies

The diverse changes associated with growth and accretion have created, enlarged, and/or made more complex the following kinds of groups in universities and colleges:

- More and more specialized departments, colleges, and professional schools with solid institutional places and identities; more inclusive aggregations (physical sciences, life sciences, social sciences, and humanities) also sometimes regard themselves as groups with interests.

- More heterogeneous groups of students (undergraduate, graduate, professional) with subdivisions among these by areas of study. Affirmative action and other diversifying policies and trends have added gender, race, ethnic group, sexual preference, and physical disabilities to the mix.

- Groups of ancillary personnel such as temporary appointees, teaching assistants, and research assistants.

- Administrative support staff created by expansion of schools, departments, library services, and the administrative apparatus generally.

- Staff associated with student services—housing, financial aid, student advising, counseling, psychotherapy, and medical care.

- Expansion of numbers of administrative offices of admission, human resources, mailing services, and so on.

- Administrative officers (budget, development, athletics, alumni relations, labor relations, public relations, government relations, and technology transfer).

- *Within* all of these groupings one observes, finally, a spread of orientation of political dispositions—loners, loyalists, conservatives, progressives, and activists—thus complicating the group picture on any campus. Union members, union supporters, those indifferent to unions, and those antagonistic to unions provide additional bases for division. Also of special interest are coalitions of faculty, students, and others who press anti–hate speech and other "politically correct" practices and points of view, as well as those who oppose these pressures on grounds of academic freedom (Bowen and Schwarz 2005).

To call all of these "constituencies" is perhaps misleading, because most of them have only latent "class consciousness" and are politically inactive most of the time. At the same time, they are (or should be) in the line of sight of sensitive administrators as groups to be taken into account or consulted when appropriate. They are sometimes activated in periods of budget preparation and are politically mobilizable on critical occasions (e.g., staff layoffs or sharp increases in tuition). More subtly, many college and university employees regard themselves as "citizens" of an organization that has traditionally liked to think of and advertise itself as an enlightened and humane employer—unlike some businesses—and as a "good place to work." This is a nice reputation to have and to cultivate, but at the same time it can be a source of expectations on the part of employees about how they will be treated as well as greater sensitivity to feelings of being ill treated. This kind of reputation—eroded as it may be in practice—may also encourage the subtle progression from privilege → right → entitlement in employees' expectations, which makes accommodating them more difficult.

External Constituencies

Many external constituencies reach into the past and persist as meaningful groups in colleges' and universities' political environments.

- The "town" side of "town–gown" relations presents a long history of ambivalence toward colleges and universities, liking them for the jobs and prestige they bring to the community but not liking them for their rowdy students, their acquisition of tax-free land, their snobbishness toward "townies," their contributions to traffic congestion and human crowding, and, more recently, their environment-threatening research activities.

- Parents of students, a latent constituency that appreciates colleges and universities for their contribution to their children's occupational success and social status. Despite the reputed death of *in loco parentis,* this constituency also expects these institutions to help keep their children out of mischief and sometimes blames them when their children bring home failing grades, rebellious attitudes, and arrest records. One potent channel of unwanted public pressure on higher education institutions is the practice of outraged parents complaining to state legislators, who then "raise questions" and embarrass administrators.

- Alumni and loyal others, a cultivated constituency valued for their sentimentality, moral support, cheerleading, and financial contributions, but also a constituency that sometimes takes an intrusive interest in the institution, especially its athletic fortunes. Loyal alumni often romanticize their own student days as they remember them—or think they remember them. Because of this they sometimes resist change, including diversification of students and faculty. Three quarters of a century ago Hutchins asserted that alumni played "a weird and often terrifying role," and he proclaimed them "the most reactionary element in the constituencies" (1936: 22, 23). Decades later, Kerr also identified alumni as forces of conservatism (1963: 102–3). As a general rule, alumni loyalties are stronger and more strongly cultivated in private than public institutions, stronger in residential than in nonresidential colleges, and stronger in four-year institutions than community colleges.

- Interested groups such as agriculture, business, and medicine, which have taken an interest in and influenced vocational and preprofessional programs of colleges and universities. Mentioning these opens up the enormous area of the relations of business and higher education, to which I will give sustained attention in chapter 3.

- A small but palpable minority of the population that is perpetually curious about academic life, consumes academic novels and movies, and takes a special interest in administrative and faculty eccentricities and scandals such as spouse-stealing and spouse-swapping.

- Finally, a diffuse "public" that permeates dialogue and discussion among university officials. It is difficult to include this as a constituency because its referent is often so vague; nobody knows exactly what or who "the public" is. In moving through policy circles in my university over the years, I have constantly heard statements such as "How will this fly with the public?" or "This is certainly not acceptable to the public," without specifying the referent. I mention this "force" both because of its frequent invocation and because of its rhetorical potency. In many ways imagined groups can be stronger than identifiable groups, largely because imagination observes fewer limits and checks than perception.

As additional external constituencies I mention those that derive from two forces: those responsible for subsidizing and otherwise supporting the university (and have led to much of its accretion), and social groups and movements in the larger society that identify colleges and universities as special targets of interest.

- Legislatures, executive state officials, and governing boards that might be considered either internal or external but from the standpoint of those responsible for administering college and university campuses have been the source of most revenue for state institutions, and constitute the ultimate authority for their management. They are or should be constantly on the radar screen for administrators. Later I will expand on the topic of public accountability.

- Private donors. In a way it is odd to mention this group as a meaningful constituency, because of college and university insistence on autonomy and discretion when receiving gifts. In practice, however, private donors do have interests in naming chairs (and on occasion have attempted to influence who is appointed to those chairs) and in naming and designating programs and directions of research according to their interests (Korean studies, Arab studies). In my own history as fund-raiser for the Center for Advanced Study in the Behavioral Sciences at Stanford, I experienced a recurrent struggle between a principle of complete discretion in spending support monies (on my part) and some specification of targets for expenditures (on the part of individual, foundation, and government donors).

- Philanthropic foundations. Historically these have been generous to colleges and universities. In many respects the University of Chicago of the 1920s was a creature of the Rockefeller Foundation; the Carnegie Foundation was also very active. After World War II foundations aggressively supplemented the federal government in sponsoring research. University medical schools and centers have benefited especially. Minimally, this kind of granting requires financial accountability—that the funds are being spent the way they are supposed to be spent. But two other tendencies make the relationship with foundations more problematic. First, foundation support was resisted by some tradition-minded as yet another manifestation of the dominance of corporate business, long rued by commentators such as Thorstein Veblen, John Dewey, and Upton Sinclair. In 1928 Harold Laski condemned the receipt of foundation funds as "[giving] the foundations a dominating control over university life which they quite emphatically ought not to have." He added that they favored professors who are active "in putting goods into the shop window" (quoted in Geiger 1986: 168). Second, in recent decades foundations' philosophies themselves have drifted *from* a policy of supporting basic research *toward* more applied, targeted research that presumably produces more direct and useful outcomes. Some, notably the Ford Foundation, invest in promoting minority and women's education. The Robert Wood Johnson Foundation has supported "activist" research on the effects of tobacco use. These directions of foundation activity cannot be described as direct interference, because once funds are granted discretion is permitted and results are not dictated; furthermore, targeted "political" spending cannot be pushed too far without endangering foundations' tax-exempt status. Nevertheless, these applied directions, significant as money troughs, act to skew the selection and emphases of research.

- Federal research funding has been the most salient arena of expansion in the past half-century. Given impetus by the country's wars and international competition and fostered by the vast expansion of basic research agencies such as the National Science Foundation and the National Institutes of Health, this mode of funding also captured the more directly mission-oriented agencies of Labor, Defense, Energy, and Justice. Though fluctuating and with an uncertain future, federal research dollars now constitute one of the largest— sometimes *the* largest, with shrinking of state support—component of state universities' budgets.

How has this largesse become part of the accretion process? Directly, foundation and government funding has accelerated the development of research centers and institutes, which provide scientific and scholarly homes that supplement academic departments. Especially in research universities, these organized research units have developed an institutional staying power and constitute major constituencies (above, pp. 27–28).

Other important sources of organizational proliferation of institutions of higher education are more indirect. First, recipients of research funds must apply for them, and they do so *through* sponsored research offices on their campuses. These offices are accretions, and necessary ones, for they require people who know about opportunities and are experts in executing the paperwork aspects of applying. Smaller, ancillary staffs of organized research institutes also assist in gaining external funding. Recipient of funds are also subject, variably, to filing progress reports, budgetary statements, and other paperwork for the granting agencies. These requirements are a legitimate part of accounting process for those receiving funds, and all call for new offices and personnel on the part of receiving institutions.

Other effects are more indirect but perhaps more potent sources of organizational growth and headaches. When colleges and universities receive federal funds, they are perforce required to conform to *general* federal laws, policies, and guidelines. These have proved to be a major force. They were in evidence during the most active phase of affirmative action, as delegations from Health, Education, and Welfare, Labor, and other departments pressured institutions to meet guidelines, with the seldom-used but extremely potent threat of withholding or withdrawing research support. Under the same umbrella colleges and universities face barrages of requirements of review and implementation of environmental regulations, health and safety regulations, human subjects requirements, and rules relating to care and treatment of animals used in experiments.

Supplementing and giving strength to these forces are the activities of numerous social movements, most with origins in the 1960s and 1970s. I have in mind the movements on behalf of ethnic and racial minorities and women, gay and lesbian rights, as well as other movements such as animal rights, rights of human subjects, and a diversity of safety and environmental issues. These movements have had direct and indirect influences on college and university policies and activities. They have operated directly through political pressure, as well as disruption and occasional threats and action against identified scholars. More important, they have influenced federal and state governments by pushing for the enactment of laws and policies that protect or favor their causes. Government granting agencies subsequently require conformity to these laws and policies.

The bite from these pressures is that, even though they are externally imposed, the affected institutions themselves must add staff to find the problems and to fix them (health inspectors, for example, to identify dangers and risks that require expenditures to set right [Zemsky, Wegner, and Massy 2005]). Under affirmative action pressure, colleges and universities appointed affirmative-action officers and staffs. The same applies to security and safety, student and employee privacy, research regulations, administering student financial aid, audit requirements and human subjects, and the rest. These organizational additions and extensions have been called "unfunded mandates" (Barr and McClellan 2011: 1). Whatever they are called, and however legitimate the social policies from which they emanate, they still, at bottom, create accretions that add to the organizational complexity and cost of higher education enterprises.

- Other social movements and political coalitions have sought to influence university policy, curricula, public statements, and even hiring and firing practices. These have emanated from the right (religious groupings, angry government officials, and political movements such as nativism and McCarthyism) and from the left (student activists, antiwar groups), who have criticized colleges and universities for their misplaced emphases and their cozy relationships with the business and political establishments. Historically these have been sources of threats to academic freedom.

- We must note, finally, the enhanced role of the media as a constituency. Decades ago two of my sociological colleagues wrote a scholarly article entitled "Some Social Functions of Ignorance" (Moore and Tumin 1949); one main message is that if potentially concerned people or groups do not know what you are doing, your freedom is thereby increased. Once upon a time, I argue, both the public and the press remained relatively ignorant and unconcerned with colleges and universities, which were regarded as serene and valuable institutions despite their oddities and foibles. Whatever the causes—growth in size and resources as well as influence, increased consequentiality for the society, dramatic scandals, conflicts, crises, and the rise of more interested constituencies—those days are gone. Institutions of higher education, especially important and prestigious ones, have become fair game for media attention and criticism. Good reading and good circulation are made by conflicts and demonstrations, administrative perks, high faculty salaries, breaches of research ethics, wastefulness, budget expansions, and budget cuts. In the 1960s I used to tease the public information officer of the Berkeley campus, insisting that his was the only such office in the country dedicated solely to keeping the University's name *out* of the news. Pertinent to my story at the moment, all this means that the media are an extremely salient external constituency for institutions of higher education, have contributed some to internal accretion in public information and public ceremonies offices, and are a chronic source of headaches for administrators.

ACCRETION, REVENUES, AND COSTS

The changes I have grouped under the heading of accretion have enormous implications for revenues and costs of institutions of higher education. Moreover, they reveal a different picture than that depicted by some commentators. In 1920 President Lowell of Harvard remarked simply, "Of the needs of a university there is, indeed, no end" (President's Report, quoted in Geiger 1986: 56). In another characterization that was simultaneously serious and tongue-in-cheek, Howard Bowen, once the premier economist of higher education, remarked that its main principle of finance was the following: ".[I]n quest of excellence, prestige, and influence . . . each institution raises all the money it can . . . [and] spends all it raises" (1980: 20). These remarks are true enough, but if we look further we find the systemic or structural bases for these depictions. The history of mutual opportunism of givers and receivers has yielded a most diverse list of revenues: tuition and fees, state and local government appropriations, federal grants and contracts, private gifts and contracts, endowment income, sales of educational activities, auxiliary enterprises, hospital revenues, and independent operations (Cohen and Noll 1998). Each has been grafted onto universities and persisted, but each has also displayed short- and long-term vicissitudes.

On the expenditure side, colleges and universities have come in for charges of administrative bloat, excess, and irresponsibility—which multiply and intensify as tuition increases are imposed and, more generally, in hard times that call for tight budgets and economies. (Interestingly, the early twentieth century produced a similar chorus of voices after a long period of rapid growth of higher education as a whole—see Veysey 1965: 307ff.). Johnstone (2001) identified the following kinds of accusations: profligacy and waste, wrong priorities, timidity or reluctance to restructure, insensitivity to student consumers, and "overselling," even over-enrolling. I would add excessive salaries and perks for faculty and administrators. Such a list is mainly "personalized" in the form of leadership excesses and policy failures. I argue that, in addition to whatever value these assertions of the workings of Parkinson's law might have, we make much further headway in understanding administrative proliferation when we examine the long-term accumulation of diverse, high-cost, mainly legitimate, *and* systemically difficult-to-reduce budgets that stem from the logic of accretion.

ACCRETION, ACADEMIC ADMINISTRATION, AND HIGHER EDUCATION POLITICS

Given what I have said (and will say) about the ambivalent reactions to change in academia, it should come as no surprise that administration and management in higher education have recently produced a landslide of critical literature of all stripes. There are several reasons for this attention: First, administrative structures have consistently burgeoned as colleges and universities have grown; in most cases their rates of growth, however measured, exceed those of faculty and students. Second, as we have just observed, administrative costs are high. Third, long-standing prejudices about administration among academics portray administrators as unnecessary, incompetent, self-serving, and meddling. (Professor A: "What is a euphemism for 'dean'?" Professor B: "I cannot say, but what is 'dean' a euphemism for?")

I will produce my own account of the changing character of administration and academic politics, but, as a sample of assessments, I give three lines of interpretation, all consistent with Panglossian-Cassandrian logic.

Management as Science and Art

As academic administration has grown and become more complex, uncertain, *and* professionalized, a flow of specialized books on its practice has emerged. This parallels the larger flow of publications on business and industrial management in general, as well as the stream on hospital administration, reflecting similar conditions of growth in that arena. Most of these volumes take the need for a systematic approach for granted, and most are dedicated to enunciating principles and guidelines, based on the assumption that higher education needs this kind of

guidance. As such, they lean in the Panglossian direction. I simply list a
tiny sample of titles in the past decade:

> *Quantitative Approaches to Higher Education Management* (Lawrence and
> Service 1977)
>
> *Implementing Management Information Systems in Colleges and Universities*
> (McManis and Parker 1978)
>
> *Applying Corporate Management Strategies* (Fecher 1985)
>
> *The Corporate University Handbook: Designing, Managing, and Growing
> a Successful Program* (Allen 2002)
>
> *The Higher Education Manager's Handbook: Effective Leadership
> in Universities and Colleges* (McCaffery 2010)

From the numbers of books published, one can conclude that there
is a market for them. They are a subclass of a larger cascade of publications directed at corporate and organizational leaders generally
and containing hopes, promises, formulae, principles, guidelines,
maxims, strategies, and tips. They constitute a significant part of the
"corporatization" of higher education, to which I will return in detail
in chapter 3.

Administration as Threat to Academic Culture

A second class of publications notices the same ballooning and system-
ization of managerial thinking but condemns them as the conquest of
forces leading to the ruination of academic values and the institutions
that embody them. Again, a sample of titles reveals the impulse:

> *The McDonaldization of Higher Education* (Hayes and Wynyard 2002)
>
> *Academic Capitalism: Politics, Policies and the Entrepreneurial University*
> (Slaughter and Leslie 1997)
>
> *University, Inc.: The Corporate Corruption of Higher Education* (Washburn
> 2005)
>
> *The University in Chains: Confronting the Military-Industrial-Radical
> Complex* (Giroux 2007)

Such publications are also numerous, and they confirm that the market for
dread and gloom is as vital as the market for success in a brave new world.

Administration as Parkinsonian

Another variant of Cassandrian thinking is that administration itself is a juggernaut, either self-generating by some internal logic or the result of willful and aggrandizing administrators. A recent interpretation along these lines is a volume by a senior professor of political science at the Johns Hopkins University published by the Oxford University Press (Ginsburg 2011). Its message is also carried by its title: *The Fall of the Faculty: The Rise of the All-Administrative University and Why it Matters.*

Ginsberg's starting point is the rapid growth of administrators and staff in the past decades, documented and always compared with the lesser rates of growth in regular faculty. He interprets this as "administrative bloat," a radical decline of faculty power over decisions that affect them, and an erosion of academic emphases. He rejects structural explanations for this, such as (a) the demand for more administration occasioned by growth in size of student bodies and faculties, (b) the mandates and record-keeping demands by governments and accrediting agencies, and (c) the power vacuum created by faculty unwillingness to engage in administration and joint governance.

Instead, Ginsberg regards the expansion as the initiative if not the power grabbing of administrators themselves. Headings in the book's chapters are "meetings, retreats, and conferences," "planning, mostly unnecessary," "image polishing and fund-raising," "administrative shirking," "administrative squandering," "corruption," "administrative theft," "insider deals," and "plagiarism and academic fraud." Most of his "data" under these headings are anecdotal, the explanations are personalized, and the tone is condemnatory.

The Structural Alternative

I take all three of these approaches—administration as systematic and scientific, administration as corrupting, administration as insidious—as more symptomatic than truthful, containing partial insights at best. Instead, I offer an interpretation of the changed structure of governance as mainly *structural* and *systemic* in character. Under "structure of governance" I include size, complexity, new management styles, conflict, crises, and crisis management. These changes are to be assigned to the long-term multiplication of functions, structures, and internal and external constituencies. A corollary is that no one class or group of agents— administrators, faculty, students, trustees, outside parties—is especially more venal or blameworthy than others, despite the abundance of accusatory literature on all sides. Here, in capsule, are the ingredients of this analysis:

First, I have already presented the argument that both the size and complexity of administration is, above all, a consequence of accretion. Growth has a quantitative aspect, but when the university takes on a new function, it builds a structure to implement that function. That structure requires people, and those people require salaries and wages. Additional costs are incurred in coordinating the diverse structures, and any external regulation of the universities activities call for internal, paid officers to be on the lookout for potential violations, and, if discovered, internal paid activities to correct them.

Second, as I have also demonstrated, the growth of structures produces a proliferation of mostly latent but significant internal constituencies. External philanthropists, donors, and agencies of research support also have interests expressed in explicit or implication expectations about how their recipient institutions carry out activities associated with their support. If you add these to the long list of standing constituencies, you have a virtual minefield of sensitive groups. This dual growth—internal and external constituencies—was captured in the following characterization of the role of the leader of a contemporary university: "In the 1970s and 1980s, the internal role of the president, leading this complex organization, turned outward" (Darden and Duderstadt 2009: 2).

Even more: because the university is and is regarded as a special moral institution, it is in a position to be attacked *on fundamental moral grounds* for any false move, such as excessive salaries, personal misconduct, steep hikes in tuition, violence on campus, usually identified in the media and by angry groups of citizens, taxpayers, and public officials. Henry Rosovsky, former Dean of Harvard, attempted to capture this general phenomenon by characterizing all these constituencies and groups as "owners" (1990). Others have spoken of multiple stakeholders. Both lines of analysis are on track, but I would carry those terms further and speak of a vast array of actual and latent groupings that swing irregularly into action—most often passionate action—when a situation in the university arouses them.

Several years ago the chancellor of the Berkeley campus formed a special committee of administrators and faculty members; it was named the "Committee on Surprises" in response a public relations crisis occasioned by campus's handling of the SARS epidemic of 2002–2003. The campus had cancelled a summer program for East Asian students for public health reasons, but universities and politicians in those countries attacked this action as an insensitive cultural "slap." The situation spilled over into antagonism from Asian American alumni groups as well, some of which were significant donors to the campus. The committee was meant to analyze the occasions for institutional surprises and, if possible, identify and predict looming surprises for the campus. It was a temporary committee, but during its life I, as a member, undertook to write a theoretical and historical essay on "Surprises at Berkeley" over the past four decades. In reflecting on the subject, I defined a "surprise"—the term also might have been "political crisis"—as follows: "an [event or situation] that arises *in relation to a definite social context of groups that have explicit or implicit normative expectations about how he university should be conducting itself"* (Smelser 2010: 82). The actual process of crisis creation is something like the following: "[d]ifferent [interested] constituencies construct stories, or narratives, about who should go to college, what should be taught, the social obligations of institutions, and the proper way to make decisions" (Birnbaum and Shushok 2001: 74–75). A crisis becomes more severe if two or more of these constituencies come into conflict with one another on the same issue; this situation creates a more complex conflict situation for administrators, who then face the likelihood of alienating *some* group or groups, no matter what decision and line of action—even a compromise—that they might take.

The contemporary, massive literature on the presidency and the management of higher education—much of which is written by battle-scarred past presidents—has produced several themes. Expectably, the jobs of leading and managing are claimed to be harder because presidents have more things to do in institutions that have grown in size, complexity, and sources of external support. Surveys show that presidents spend more of their time on campus crises, fund-raising, and management than on academic matters (American Council on Education 2007). Beyond that is the theme, often accompanied by some moaning, that the really great statesmen of past eras—Eliot of Harvard, Butler of Columbia, Brewster of Yale, indeed Kerr of the University of California—are no more. Current leaders are more managerial than presidential. They fail to enunciate grand visions of the university and to make profound statements on the political and moral issues of the day. Themes include "being many things to many people," spending all their time in courting and pleasing potential funders, spending an inordinate amount of time in preventing, fending off, and managing crises, and defending the institution when it is criticized. Nelson's "key question" for presidents is "[A]re [they] . . . able to locate, to define wisely, and articulate publicly, and to urge consensus toward a center—educational, philosophical and moral in nature— for their institutions and for their campus constituents?" (2007: xxvi). Though sometimes confused, the literature is right. The fragmentation of leadership roles is, I submit, a direct function of all the consequences of accretion that I have identified. The reluctance (with exceptions) to speak out on the big issues arises *first* from the fact that so many of those issues are controversial and *second* from the fact that the audience of interested constituencies is both large and diverse. Almost *any* strong, general pronouncement is likely to offend *some* group. One past president advised, simply, "[Y]ou may be attacked from any quarter at any time by any one of your many constituencies" (Flawn 1990: xi). Chose your analogy, because all are correct: there are more feathers to be ruffled, more toes waiting to be stepped on, more eggs that have to be walked on, more tulip fields through which one must tiptoe. It is often more advisable to say nothing— or perhaps better, sweet nothings—than to speak one's mind forcefully. I am describing this augmentation of timidity not so much as a function of the changed personalities or faults of leaders but rather in the changed *structural contexts* affecting the institutions they lead. Finally, I interpret the long-term decline in length of tenure in office of presidents (Padilla 2004) as an expression of the evolution of more, more complex, and more demanding constituencies.

Implications for Shared Governance

As is well known, self-governance (now evolved into "shared governance") is regarded by university faculties as one of the most treasured aspects of their heritage. It is also the subject of a mythology of its own past; Keller speaks of a myth of faculty that "there was once an Edenic time in U.S. history when a condition of faculty control and Athenian self-government [existed] on most campuses" (1983: 31). The phrase "shared governance" is still the major legitimizing symbol for assertions of faculty influence and power.

My overall assessment of faculty participation and shared governance coincides with that of my late colleague, Martin Trow. Despite enormous variation in structure and process among categories of institutions, "academic senates and committees in the leading universities still gain the willing and largely unrewarded participation of active and leading scholars and scientists in the process of governance by consultation" (1990: 105). He also judged the leavening influence of faculty governance to be largely positive. I would add that its value stems largely from the fact that the faculty voice is the conscience of the university, the strongest source of affirmation of its fundamental values.

Valuable as it is, faculty governance has experienced a certain withering and ineffectiveness in the past decades. One depiction, though somewhat overdrawn, identifies the standard problems:

> The number of faculty members who take part in senate and committee deliberations is usually small relative to the number eligible to do so. Moreover, the same faces appear and reappear among the participants, with few being the campus's most successful scholars and teachers. The faculty comes to regard governance activities as the province of mere politicians, who speak for themselves only and are therefore unable to overcome centrifugal forces. At the same time, cynicism becomes the symptom among administrators. They go

through the motions of collaborative decision making because bylaws
or good politics require it, but they have no respect for these processes
and pay as little heed to them as is compatible with a sullen peace.
(Weingartner 1996: 21)

Insofar as these characterizations have merit, I regard the main trends
that have led to this transformation and decline of shared governance as
the following:

- The fact of steady and expanding growth of full-time administrators
  and managers, whose more or exclusive preoccupation is with managing. It seems self-evident that the relationship between collegial
  participation and bureaucratic formality has steadily evolved in
  favor of the latter as a principle of governance over the decades.

- The fact that those classes of managers find multiple-constituency inputs to their work a necessary part of their scene. In particular, con-
  tinuous and mandatory faculty consultation, often ritual, is essential
  for administrators to maintain support on the part of faculty; one of
  the most damaging faculty accusations an administrator faces is that
  "we were not consulted." Faculty thus typically regard participation
  in governance as a sacred right; administrators often regard it as a
  necessary nuisance.

- The fact that more and more administrators are recruited from
  nonfaculty, often managerial backgrounds creates a situation of
  even greater cultural distance and antagonism between faculty and
  administration. This can only harden stereotypes that administrators are small-minded dullards and faculty are spoiled, arrogant
  troublemakers.

- The fact that participation in faculty governance is often simultaneously voluntary and time-consuming. Some high-level faculty
  governance positions are rewarded with time off from teaching and
  stipends, but most are not.

- The costs of joining a voluntary army become higher when other
  lines of activity— conducting and publishing research, consulting at
  high levels, striving for prizes and other recognition—are typically
  more enjoyable and rewarding than "senate work."

- The competing demands on faculty life, combined with the academic calendar, make for great delays and inefficiency in faculty
  participation in governance. Faculty teach, give oral exams, attend

conferences, travel to conferences and conventions, and consult. They are also reluctant to schedule meetings in the summer and during winter, spring, and Thanksgiving "breaks." As a result, the pace of their committee work is often glacial, while administrative officials are simultaneously experiencing greater urgency. Furthermore, academic senates appear to have become even more sluggish when they have formed or consolidated into multicampus organizations to "co-govern" with multicampus administrations.

All these trends have accumulated by drift, remained largely unacknowledged, and generated few efforts at reform. This stalemate has developed because faculties are conservative, jealous, and suspicious, and because administrators know that to take initiative with respect to faculty governance is to step into a minefield. My own view is that, given *both* the value and indispensability of shared governance *and* its deterioration, the only proper course is for administration and faculty to confront one another openly and frankly about their values and frustrations, about what is working and not working in shared governance, and initiate joint efforts to diagnose problems, identify points of vulnerability, and attempt to overhaul and streamline archaic structures.

ACCRETION AND ACADEMIC STRATIFICATION

Earlier I referred to the production of new categories of teaching and research personnel, ancillary to the "establishment" tenure-track faculty and relegated to second-class citizenship. Now I return to that theme and tie it more specifically to the process of accretion.

The first point to be made is that colleges and universities are wonderfully inventive in producing unequal categories, perhaps the most accomplished of all institutions in this art. This is the "you name it, we'll rank it" phenomenon. Becher remarked that "[one] of the striking features of academic life is that nearly everything is graded in more or less subtle ways" (1989:56). The remark has its ironic side, because so many advocates and defenders of higher education stress its consistency with and promotion of democratic values. Despite the irony, the tendency is endemic. Within the professorial ranks we have acting assistant, assistant, associate (with and without tenure), full professor, supplemented by named chairs, above-scale appointments, and university professors—a status spectrum extending from apprenticeship to supergalactic eminence. "Stars" rank higher than "deadwood" (Gumport 1991). Faculty who give essay exams look down their noses at the "multiple-choice" crowd. Some faculty in "mainstream" departments look down on those who teach in physical education, ethnic studies, or gay and lesbian studies (D'Augelli 1991). Some faculty members in the liberal arts look down on their professional school colleagues for not being truly academic and intellectual (Duderstadt 2000: 106). Schools (medical, law, business) strive for separate salary schedules, reflecting market demand but also creating new ranks. Within departments and disciplines individual faculty strive for different kinds of advantage— rank, salary, relief from committee assignments, size of teaching load, graduate-versus-undergraduate teaching—none of which is exclusively a status symbol, but all of which connote status, advantage, and differential distribution of perks and influence. Even within the ranks of non-tenure-track appointees, status distinctions hold between full-time and part-time appointees, those giving for-credit and those giving non-credit courses, and those giving "transfer" courses over those giving "vocational status" courses (Kemperer 1991). Ranking systems, finally, set the stage for endless struggles to attain valued positions. Bourdieu put it as follows: "[T]he university . . . is . . . the locus of a struggle to determine the conditions and the criteria of legitimate membership and legitimate hierarchy" (1988: 11).

In the remarks that follow I trace three additional lines of stratification that are closely related to accretion—prestige stratification among institutions, special issues of stratification in multicampus systems, and stratification among departments and disciplines.

Institutional Prestige

General prestige rankings among institutions are as old as institutions themselves. In the American case they have broken down into subcategories such as the long-established private universities (notably the Ivies but coming to include Chicago, Stanford, MIT, and Cal Tech); flagship universities in the states, some in competition for prestige with the major privates; four-year private liberal arts colleges (Swarthmore, Carleton Oberlin, etc.). A critical moment in the history of ranking was the formation of the Association of American Universities in 1915, which included the elite privates and publics at the time, and while the AAU has grown to some sixty institutions, that association still signifies status. Even the Carnegie classification of universities and colleges, originally intended as a device to render the diversity of institutions intelligible, has evolved into a "yardstick of prestige" for striving institutions (Brewer et al. 2002: 47), with some institutions seeking changes in their classification status. State universities and community colleges also seek status and reputation.

Formal and publicized rankings of research universities began with the study by Hughes (1925) nearly a century ago and have developed through more elaborate renditions up to the present efforts of the National Research Council (Ostriker and Kuh 2003). More recently, international systems of university rankings have evolved, the most conspicuous being those of the Shanghai Jiao Tong University and the *Times Higher Education Supplement*. Criteria have proliferated, but the most constant are reputations for quality of research and quality of programs of graduate education. I note several features of these periodic ranking systems:

- Administrators and faculties are keenly aware of them. They follow them closely and cite them selectively and ambivalently. It has been said that when the rankings appear, 20 percent of the ranked institutions throw a cocktail party and the remaining 80 percent criticize the methodology. The reasons for this high salience, in my estimation, is that the rankings serve as tangible, simplified, but available symbols in a very precarious but highly important world of competition for donors, legislative support, research funds, and student enrollments. This is a general principle: importance plus ambiguity yields simplified symbols, and simplified symbols become reality. These reified symbols, finally, also become objects of simultaneous love and hate. This combination of features also accounts for why "it is unrealistic to imagine that complaining about rankings and lamenting their popularity will do anything to slow their growth and appeal" (Wildawsky 2010: 245). One confirming anecdote tells the story: Decades ago, when I was chairing an outside evaluation team for the Sociology Board of Studies at the University of California at Santa Cruz, I was meeting with the faculty members as one part of the evaluation. At a given moment one faculty member demanded that I give my opinion as to where Santa Cruz sociology ranked nationally. I refused to take the bait, but the demand for my opinion spread and became a din. I finally capitulated and said that in my estimation it would be difficult to envision a ranking of Santa Cruz in the top three dozen at that time. I thought this a considered and honest—even generous—response, but I was nearly driven from the campus twice, first for not uttering it, and then for uttering it.

- The rankings are methodologically vulnerable, largely because they have relied so highly on reputational surveys (a partial and questionable measure), because—focusing on disciplines—they seldom measure and therefore neglect interdisciplinary work, because halo effects operate (nonexistent departments at Harvard are said to receive high ratings), and because different measures yield such different outcomes in ranking that interested parties can read them selectively. *Any* institution can find *something* on which they rank higher than others. Simple changes in methodologies, moreover, yield strange results. To cite only one example, some changes in methodology in the rankings of the *Times Higher Education Supplement* in 2007 "contribute[d] to Stanford University's drop from number 6 to 19, the National University of Mexico's plunge from 74 to 192, and National University of Singapore's decline from 19 to 33" (Wildawsky 2010: 226).

- The surveys do much to concretize long-standing reference points for institutional emulation and striving. Harvard, Yale, Princeton, Berkeley, Michigan, and Stanford all look at one another most; Iowa looks at Michigan and Wisconsin; Oklahoma looks at Texas; other University of California campuses look toward Berkeley, UCLA, and UC San Diego. Swarthmore, Sarah Lawrence, Wellesley, and Smith look at one another.

- We observe, finally, a certain irony in the prestige rankings of institutions. They are remarkably stable over time. Over the long hall we can identify institutional risings and fallings—UC San Diego, Stanford, Northwestern, Johns Hopkins, Clark University—but the general picture is that the leading universities continue to lead, and others chase behind. The story is one of stability, but this does not seem to dampen the competitive drive of wannabes to move upward in the rankings (Tuchman 2009). One might call this scene both a tragedy and a comedy.

Back to the main point: the three major sources of accretion in the twentieth century have been philanthropic activity among foundations, directed research funding on the part of federal agencies, and investment and collaboration from corporate sources in the University. The activities of these external sources have reinforced—better, exaggerated—the institutional rankings. The rich get richer; they dominate in the distribution of research support. The reasons for this differ by source but are basically similar. Foundations want to make maximum impact in their giving, and for that reason choose the important institutions; there are some equalizing programs, but these are outweighed by the dominant principle. Federal granting agencies are motivated to ensure quality in their giving, and by doing so they help protect their own reputations. Guided by these forces, and by peer reviewing from experts who are both instructed and inclined to stress "quality" in their evaluations, their flow is also to the most prestigious research institutions. Some counter-pressures are noticed, such as efforts by some administrative leaders and politicians to secure earmarked research support for institutions in their own regions and states—we might call this "intellectual pork"—but these forces remain secondary (Rosenzweig 1998: 41). Business and industry, finally, in their competition for innovation and market position, go after the highest quality in their investments and via this simple motive favor the top institutions. All these forces are also discouraging to the wannabee strivers, but this does not seem to diminish their drive for grants, recognition, and status.

The preoccupation with institutional prestige has spread, with perhaps even more vigor, in the ranking of undergraduate institutions and programs. These are more popular than the general research and graduate-training rankings, represented as they are in magazines (especially the famous *U.S. News and World Report* ranking, begun in 1983 and expanding thereafter) and in numerous published handbooks and guidebooks. The most recent *U.S. News* "Ultimate College Guide" (2011) is 1,760 pages in length, complete with rankings of hundreds of colleges on eleven critical factors, discussion of majors, and lined pages for note-taking at the end. These rankings, too, have a history of both fascination and vilification. The fascination is overdetermined, driven by the anxious preoccupation of parents ambitious for their children and children ambitious for themselves, both of whom know the "value added" of a college education and the greater value imparted by a prestigious degree; by secondary schools, especially independents, who seek to gain in prestige and in capacity to recruit their own students according to how well they "place" their graduates; by colleges themselves, who see gains in recruitment resulting from their prestige rankings; by the ranking publications, whose reports enjoy brisk sales; and by employers who continuously look for tangible evidence of talent in their recruitment. The rankings are a shorthand device for all these groups, and they compel their attention, even though charges of inaccuracy and methodological shortcomings continue to fly. Publishers of rankings, on their part, continue to refine their methodologies in the face of criticisms as a way of strengthening their credibility (Wildawsky 2010).

Multicampus Systems and Stratification

The growth of multicampus systems of administration is one of the major institutional developments in the last half of the twentieth century. It was stimulated by a combination of several forces: (a) The enormous growth of state higher education in the post–World War II boom, combined with the evident limitations of the strategy of expanding the numbers enrolled in states' flagship institutions (the University of Rome, when it was still a huge single campus, never seemed a viable model for this country). Some flagship institutions did expand considerably (Minnesota and Ohio State, for example); others (California, for example) set caps on enrollments of some campuses and relied on the expansion of other existing campuses and the creation of new ones. (b) Because public campuses were dependent in important ways on the same general sources of support (mainly state governments, but some local jurisdictions as well), the pressure to regulate competition for resources became more salient (especially in tough budgetary times) and the issues of coordination (e.g., unnecessary duplication of programs and contending with competing demands) also became more urgent. The rise of multicampus systems as an intermediary between individual campus system and states' political authorities became the preferred institutional answer to these new exigencies. While extremely diverse with respect to inclusiveness of different categories of institutions, modes of governance, and autonomy from the state (see Johnstone 1999), they were widely adopted, so that by the end of the century, 80 percent of the nation's students were enrolled in institutions that were part of a system (Gaither 1999). From their multiple aspects, I choose a few problems of institutional stratification that were created and highlighted in these systems.

The forces of stratification and competition in these systems take different forms. For those (e.g., Texas, New York) with multiple types of institutions (research universities, four-year colleges, community colleges), these forces are in one respect muted, because in many areas these types *cannot*, by law and policy, compete, for example, for Ph.D. programs and professional schools, because only a few institutions can, by law and policy, have them. Competition remains, however, in other areas, especially share of state resources. Coordination in these heterogeneous institutions, on the other hand, is more difficult; because of their diversified character, uniform policies are more difficult to come by.

When multicampus organizations comprehend only one segment (e.g., the state of California, which has separate systems for research universities, state universities, and community colleges), the constituent campuses of a system are comparable in functions. The segments are themselves ranked in relation to one another (above, pp. 13–14), and *within* each segment the constituent campuses are also ranked by dint of different histories, past successes, and differences in levels of support. Within such systems competition takes a distinctive form. Those regarded as most prestigious (typically, the flagship and other long-standing campuses) tend to argue from the vantage point of the cultural value of excellence; those lower in hierarchy tend to argue from the vantage point of the cultural values of equality, equity, and commonality of citizenship. With elite institutions fighting to retain advantage and keep what they have, and with other campuses fighting for new programs and installations to enhance *their* status and quality, one inevitable consequence is the pressure for more accretion, in this case out of persistent feelings of relative deprivation. Jack Peltason, onetime chancellor of the University of California, Irvine, is reported to have jested, "If Chuck Young [chancellor of UCLA] has a lollipop, I want a lollipop just like his." Furthermore and finally, the process governing the outcomes of the competition relies as much on the persuasiveness and political influence of presidents and chancellors as it does on rational organizational calculation.

One other observation regarding multicampus centers is in order. Because they are often remote from the individual campuses they govern, because they have different organizational exigencies from campuses, and because they are often regarded as the source of interference as well as assistance to campuses, they operate at a cultural disadvantage. After all, it is the physically situated campus to which students apply; it is on individual campuses on which they lead their student lives and to which they build up sentiments and loyalties; and it is individual campuses from which they graduate and to which they are asked to donate as alumni and alumnae. Faculty institutional loyalties, tattered as they might have become, lie at the campus level.

Multicampus organizations have no students or faculties, only administrators, who are always targets for ambivalence. One experienced observer ventured the opinion that "the system presidency [chancellorship] is the least stable of higher education presidencies and often the least satisfying chief executive position" (Kaufman,1993: 128). They have little or no romance or sentimental mythology about them. General legitimizing symbols are difficult to come by; the notions of "one university" or "a single university" are typically regarded by campuses as inaccurate and possibly mischievous myths at best, and illegitimate claims to influence and power at worst. The work of multicampus centers is regarded as helpful and facilitative of campus life, responsible as they are for dealing directly with boards of trustees and government bodies and taking the inevitable political heat, but they are also blamed for failing in those activities. And they are equally often regarded as invasive and duplicative of campus activities. It seems to be the nature of the beast that multicampus centers are organizationally essential but culturally anomalous.

Prestige among Disciplines

Competition among the disciplines works itself out in many settings:

- In universities themselves. Departments, as maximizers of prestige (Balderston 1974) assert their worth, their importance, and their priorities to deans and higher administrators, especially at budget-setting time, often citing national rankings and levels of research support generated (Pfeffer and Slancik 1974). They may also demean the worth of competitors.

- Among relevant publics. Wider perception of a discipline's worth as an intellectual enterprise is an asset in seeking funding from foundations and government granting agencies and in election to the rosters of honoring groups such as the American Philosophical Society and the Guggenheim Foundation.

- Among themselves. Lord Rutherford remarked that "[all] science is either physics or stamp collecting" (quoted in Duderstadt 2000: 123). In the social sciences, which I know best, status is often claimed on the basis of how "scientific" the discipline is in relation to some vision of the natural sciences. Psychology lays claim to prestige because of its "scientific" experimentalism, economics because of its rigorous theoretical structure and its mathematical and quantitative emphases. The other social sciences seem "softer" on these criteria, but they promote their own greater "realism." Within disciplines experimental psychology trumps clinical, personality, and above all "humanistic" psychology on these grounds; econometrics trumps labor economics and economic development; and in sociology demography presses its own rigor in relation to areas such as family and educational sociology. To outsiders all these may seem little more than idle status games, but they matter directly and indirectly in intra-university struggles, competition for resources, political voice, and general esteem.

The last half-century of accretion occasioned by the activities of foundations, the federal government, and industry has had profound implications for the well-being and status of disciplines and classes of disciplines. We recall that the main stimuli for their support of universities have been wars, other kinds of military competition, international economic competition, and the health of the population. The physical sciences, life sciences, engineering, and computer and informational sciences have received the greatest largesse from federal granting agencies. Many private foundations have placed health and environmental concerns—both stressing science and technology—at the top of their agendas. Corporate linkages have rewarded biomedical and bioengineering sciences. By comparison with the physical and life sciences, the social sciences have been starvelings, but they, too, have benefited. The National Science Foundations has smaller grant programs for many of them, and many foundations and government mission agencies (e.g., the Departments of Justice, Labor, and Health and Human Services) have stressed social problems and the social knowledge requisite for dealing with them. The true victims have been the humanities (for an extreme, Cassandrian view, see Readings 1996). Already somewhat undervalued historically, they have not caught attention from private foundations, with notable exceptions such as the Mellon Foundation. They are not represented in the federal government's military, defense, and environmental research expenditures. They have had to rely on the much smaller, erratically funded, and politically vulnerable National Endowment for the Humanities and National Endowment for the Arts.

This differential largesse has occasioned major shifts in resources, status, and influence within the receiving institutions. Salary differentials have been further skewed toward the sciences and some professional schools (Engell and Dangerfield 2005); so have perks such as teaching relief, summer salaries, research assistants, postdoctoral programs, and travel funds. Administrators treasure and favor the big scientific research institutes that bring in large grants with large overhead costs. All this means that, both absolutely and relatively, the natural sciences are gorged, the social sciences are fed, and the humanities are starved. If one adds to these effects the radical decline over the decades of college majors in the humanities (Hacker and Dreifus 2010) in relation to more practical and vocational majors such as computer sciences, business, and environmental studies, one can truly appreciate the validity of the heralded "crisis of the humanities," proclaimed by several scholars to be a "global crisis" recently in the magazine *Oxford Today* (Nussbaum 2011; Bate 2011; Blakemore 2011). Moreover, these developments justify apprehensions that the "idea of the university"—that is, the search for truth and imparting the truth in <u>all</u> relevant areas of knowledge—is seriously compromised by developments in the past half-century. True, organizational inertia continues to assert itself. Colleges and universities have been reluctant simply to scrap small and struggling departments, and they continue to subsidize the humanities, but the overall decline is real and grave. The humanities resent their decline and their poverty, and the "fat cat" disciplines sometimes resent the subsidization.

The politics of the university do not escape the effects of these shifts. Those who have greater power to bring resources to the university perforce gain louder voices with perpetually resource-hungry administrators. And those who have suffered in resources and status in the universities' supposed "company of equals" have tended to become radicalized. A half-century ago, Kerr could pronounce, cryptically, "scientists affluent, humanists militant" (1963: 60). More than one observer (e.g., Zemsky, Wegner, and Massy 2005) has noted that the voices of humanists are most highly represented and loudest in the cascades of protest against the devastation of higher education by commercialization, marketization, managerialism, and money.

Those political reactions are understandable as expressions of the alienation and reminiscences of those who see their world as impoverished and shrinking. I would also speculate that the effects of these changes have spread to the more purely academic realm. In the 1980s a family of somewhat interrelated intellectual movements came upon the scene under the headings of deconstructionism and postmodernism (for a general source, see Zima 2002). This intellectual movement had many facets, but I call to your attention one of its ingredients: it was explicitly antiscience in import. That ingredient is at the heart of constructionism itself, namely, the assertion that abstract entities (such as the idea of the self) and general—including scientific—explanations are bogus because they involve the fallacy of essentialism. In fact, goes the argument, they are collective constructions, often serving the interests of the powerful in society. The science-as-construction theme became the butt of anti-postmodernist jokes about the postmodernist who refused to get his car repaired because the broken-down carburetor was a social construction, and the postmodernist who hurled himself out of a thirty-story window to prove that the principle of gravity was a social construction. These are unkind caricatures, but it is true that one of general features of the postmodernist thrust is a radical epistemological relativism that is anti-scientific and antigeneralizing in its intellectual import.

It is also true that the postmodernistic impulse spread differentially. It captured the attention of humanists most of all—in language studies, English, and history, for example. In the social sciences it invaded sub-fields often regarded as "soft," such as cultural anthropology, history of science, gender and feminist studies, that is, areas with less solid "scientific" commitments. Experimental psychologists and economists, to say nothing of natural scientists, scarcely noticed the movement, and when they did they usually dismissed it as antipositivistic nonsense. In this interpretation I acknowledge that these thoughts are my own speculations. But I would also add that the obscurantist language of postmodernism did little service to those, including humanists espousing the movement, who were often dismissed as being both incomprehensible and nihilistic. (Q: "What do you get when you cross a Mafia agent with a postmodernist?" A: "An offer you can't understand."). To this light note I would like to add a serious but controversial intellectual conclusion. The intellectual value of the postmodernist movement must be decided, above all, on its own intellectual terms even though I personally regard it, in the longer run, as an unproductive dead end in terms of intellectual results. But the movement and the reactions to it are clearly also comprehensible as expressions in the context of the increasing inequality among disciplines and reactions to that inequality.

THREE

Contemporary Trends

DIAGNOSES AND CONDITIONAL PREDICTIONS

Higher Education in America is in trouble.
Deep trouble.

Rosenstone 2005

In the first chapter I presented a general and systematic—but peculiar—
view of how institutions of higher education, with emphasis on
universities, change over time. In the second I traced out as many implications as I could from this account—implications for cost, administration, conflict, political processes and stratification. This third chapter
takes a further step, assessing recent trends and what they bode for the
future, *but in the context of conditions that have been established historically.*
With respect to the relation of these trends to structural accretion—
the organizing theme of the first two chapters—this chapter presents
a mixed picture. Some of the trends (e.g., the development of long-
distance learning) add to past accretions, some (e.g., financial stric-
tures) are made more severe because they are developing in the context
the structures deposited from past accretions, and some (e.g., faculty

unionism) are produced by multiple factors, some but not all related to accretion processes.

This chapter is the boldest of all, for two reasons: (a) there is so much disagreement as to nature, meaning, and depth of current developments, and (b) many conditions will affect the future and we cannot make accurate assumptions about most of them. I can say for certain that I will be neither rosy Panglossian nor gloomy Cassandrian, suspicious as I am about such diagnoses and solutions.

AN UNPRECEDENTED PERFECT STORM

Despite this disclaimer, I can begin by identifying a series of developments that are producing what some (e.g., Wadsworth 2005) have described as a perfect storm—a convergence of adverse trends that spell a downhill spiral and erosion at least and destruction at most of the traditions and ideals of our academic institutions. Those trends, in brief, are as follows:

- Increased global competitiveness and a suffering national and world economy, for what duration we do not know. For our country this has meant economic crisis and stagnation, unemployment, and regressive movements in the distribution of income. All institutions and all projects seem to be under pressure; educational institutions are being asked, more than ever, to contribute to the nation's competitiveness in the global economy.

- Severe and accelerating slashing of state spending on education, despite the onslaught of a "third tidal wave of students." These cuts are occasioned in large part by those mentioned economic forces, but they are aggravated by loud political voices of other claimants, all stronger political constituents than higher education, as well as the debilitating effects of taxpayer revolts or threats of them. Higher education cuts by states are easier to justify, moreover, because the negative effects are felt only further down the line than the next election (above, p. 47). These changes have harmed public institutions most and aggravated their situation in relation to the privates. Publics have responded largely by raising tuition and fees, which alarm students and parents alike and provoke bursts of public ire.

- Two disastrous recessions in a decade—the dot-com collapse of
  2001–2002 and the financial debacle of 2008—that initially hit the
  privates especially but took a heavy toll on all institutions.

- The persistence of forces that limit or reduce minority and poor students in higher education—increasing tuition without ample offsets;
  the burdens of educational loans; differential preparation in primary
  and secondary schools; class and family differences in producing
  necessary "cultural capital"; and campus climates that directly or
  indirectly discourage the less privileged. We also see a "squeeze of
  the middle" of the income distribution, who have fewer resources
  and receive fewer offsets.

- The long-term drift toward vocationalism at the expense of liberal
  learning in *all* institutions, including the spectacular rise of for-profit,
  mainly long-distance learning institutions. This is in part traceable
  to, and certainly accelerated by, new technological and job requirements, by global economic competitors, and by the aggressive practices of those competitors who are rushing, without ambivalence,
  into technology and technological training.

- The further corruption of colleges and universities by their increasing
  research collaboration with industry, which diverts faculty in its choice
  of research, skews academic values, and creates conflicts of interest.

- The conversion of colleges and universities into commercially
  oriented enterprises fighting to survive on all fronts, eroding their
  academic commitments, and creating a managerial class driven
  by values of consumerism, efficiency, downsizing, and image
  projection.

- The onward march of efforts to make institutions of higher education
  more accountable in many ways, occasioning further assaults on
  their traditional autonomy.

- The rise of online distance learning as threat to traditional
  educational formats, and the concurrent rise of for-profit, mainly
  vocational institutions based on computer learning.

- The long-term and extreme increases in temporary full-time and
  part-time faculty, which creates a huge academic proletariat and
  threatens academic tenure and academic freedom by erosion of
  protected classes.

Furthermore, many of these processes appear to be irreversible, given
the incessancy of the undermining forces. While not downplaying the

magnitude of these forces, and agreeing with some of the diagnoses, I do not share the extreme pessimism. In the remainder of this chapter I will consider in more detail some of the elements of the storm—budgetary threats and accountability; commercialization; distance education and the rise of the for-profit educational institutions; the growth of nontenure track and part-time faculty.

UNPRODUCTIVE PARADOXES: STARVATION, ACCOUNTABILITY, AND GOVERNANCE

In the decade of the 1980s, a number of trends began or converged, all of which conspired to impinge on higher education adversely and, considered together, put the system on a collision course that has yet to be faced fully. I identify the major trends as the following:

- The flow of traditional students (the 18–24 cohort) diminished, though the numbers of "nontraditionals" (older, minority, women) continued their long-term upward trend. Most of the expansion has been absorbed by the growth of community colleges and four-year institutions, and later by the exploding sector of for-profit, distance learning institutions. In large part these have been adaptations to job market changes, providing new lines of training for new service occupations.

- The leveling and sometimes decline in levels of federal research support continued the downward ebb begun in the 1970s after the halcyon days of the Sputnik-Vannevar Bush era (Slaughter and Leslie 1997) and continued in the 1990s after the end of the Cold War.

- States were beginning to question budgetary support for "their" institutions as early as the 1970s, presaging the subsequent downward trend in public funding and accelerating into a stunning decline. In 1980 the percentage of state support for public institutions of higher education was 50 percent; by 1995 the percentage had dropped to 45 percent and is still falling annually (Layzell and Caruthers 1999). Current estimates place the figure nearer to 25 percent (Lyell 2009). The quip is that "we were once state supported, then state assisted, and now we are state located." Even that now needs qualification, as many institutions—for example, Carnegie-Mellon, SUNY-Buffalo, UC San Diego—have set up programs in other countries (Berdahl 2008).

- The major response to falling state support has been to initiate a corresponding trend toward rising annual tuition rates in all institutions, but notably state-supported ones. This meant shifting the burden of support for education from funds generated by taxation to individual students and their families. The "sea change" from student grants to student loans involved a similar shift to students at the time they reach their postcollegiate years (see Potter and Chickering 1991). All these produced a general sense that college education was drifting from its traditional status as a "public good" and a responsibility of the societal community in the direction of a "private good, " in which families and students invest in the interest of advancing their well-being in the economy (getting a better job) and a higher place in the country's status-system (certification).

- In the wider world the economy remained problematical, producing a significant recession in the mid-1980s. More generally, the nation was caught up in panic over foreign economic competition, especially from Japan, which, it was argued, was becoming "Number One" (Vogel 1979). The alarm produced several interrelated developments, including efforts to mimic Japanese cultural and organizational patterns (notably Total Quality Control, but other practices as well), with corresponding assaults on American businesses and business schools (Cheit 1985) for their inefficiencies. The alarm was also a factor in the government encouragement of industry–university cooperation (below, pp. 97–99).

- Interest in accountability was already evident; in 1971 one author described it as the "in word" in American education (Hartnett 1971: 5). The impulse produced an accountability movement (some would say "accountability mania") in the 1980s and into the 1990s, affecting industry, the federal government, and state governments. This movement also occasioned an extension of the criteria of accountability to include general performance and organizational effectiveness, in addition to the traditional foci on financial accountability (spending funds on purposes for which they were intended) and legal accountability (conforming to the law in conducting organizational business).

General Consequences of Shifts in Support and Costs

From one point of view the shift from a public to a private (consumer) status might be regarded as desirable. Public education has long been touted as a democratizing influence in society, giving opportunities for those of modest backgrounds to advance themselves; since the onset of affirmative action and its variations, it has also been cast as an instrument of social justice. At the same time, researchers have pointed out that its influence on income is regressive in a specific sense. The argument is that the composition of student bodies, even in public institutions, is "loaded" in the direction of students more privileged in terms of parental income (and thus social class) and accumulated cultural capital. If these relatively advantaged students are supported from funds derived from general taxation, then poorer groups—both currently and in terms of future income—are subsidizing them, and the general effect is regressive (for comparative evidence on and evaluation of this argument, see Shavit, Arum, and Gamoran 2007). If we follow this argument, the emerging pattern of having privileged consumers pay for their children's education seems more equitable and just.

But that argument is only part of the story. Universities and colleges have long devoted some percentage of their resources to providing scholarship aid for students who could not otherwise afford to attend college. Grants and loans to minority students were driven by the same impulse. As tuition and fees for all institutions began their momentous ascent some decades ago, the problem of affording access to low-income and minority students grew correspondingly. The favored policy to counter this trend was to adopt policies (by the government and by institutions of higher education) to divert increasing amounts of funds to low-income students in the form of grants and loans, in order to keep pace with their otherwise increasing disadvantage. This pattern not only creates a continuing problem of playing "catch-up" with the disadvantages of the poor; it also disadvantaged those families who are not poor enough to qualify for need-based financial aid but not well-off enough to afford the spiraling rates of tuition and fees. Symptomatic of these developments is the drift of concern, beginning around 1980, from that of "access" to that of "affordability" (Richardson and Hurley 2005). Nevertheless, differential access for minorities remains problematical. Public attention to this issue and institutional responsiveness was highest during the rush of the affirmative action movement in the 1970s. In the following decade, attention to access was deflected by the panic over American productivity and competiveness and higher education's responsibility for improving them. Later the "backlash" against affirmative action, including political measures in several states, occasioned a further setback. And finally, the downward spiral of state support and upward spiral of private costs, unless compensated for, adversely affects minorities, especially black, Hispanic, and Native American. The net consequences of this history are that minority access remains a salient issue in the economics and politics of higher education but that progress on that front is continuously liable to backsliding.

Another consequence of the combination of reduced state support and increased fees is less tangible but nonetheless grave. That has to do with the changes in the institutional good will of families wanting to send their children to college. The immediate impact of sharp annual increases in fees is one of relative deprivation—education is getting more costly for their children, and they feel pinched, even if public education is still a bargain and if they can still "afford" it in some absolute sense. A common consequence of feeling thus deprived is to blame the immediate source—that is, those institutions that are doing the raising of prices. This also generates greater sensitivity to and criticism of real and imagined inefficiencies, administrative bloat, waste, idleness, irresponsibility, and the perks, pleasures, and soft life of college and university administrators and faculty. It also means a stronger disposition to complain about these institutions to legislators and other state government officials. Students themselves, facing these increases, also periodically demonstrate against the campuses that tell them they must pay significantly more next year. This protest is often embarrassing for campuses, particularly if they and their police crack down on protesters and escalate the conflicts. In one respect parental criticisms and student protests against campuses amount to shooting the messenger, because colleges and universities themselves are not responsible for but are the victims of reduced budgets. In fact, the interests of students' parents, students, and higher education institutions are the same in this case—to maintain or increase state support and to keep fees down—but the ire of the first two often falls on the latter.

This complex of reactions yields a vicious circle. Systematic and prolonged cutting drives educational institutions to raise their prices, especially with those that have fewer alternative sources of income such as federal research grants with overhead costs, foundation support, and private giving. The cutting also exerts pressure on institutions to sustain the quality of their work with reduced resources. Raising prices and economizing, however, are sources of irritation to student and parent consumers, who tend to expect more, not less, if they pay more. Yet the educational institutions themselves, being relatively impoverished by the cuts and politically vulnerable if they continue to hike prices, have little ability to reverse the downward spiral of external support and upward spiral of costs to their students. The "vicious" component emerges in the increased cost, increased public dissatisfaction, and increased interest on the part of state to enforce quality and efficiency while at the same time reducing support—all resulting in the decreasing autonomy of educational institutions.

Accountability, Governance, and Support

Most public institutions are creatures of and ultimately accountable to the founding and funding individual states, even though they may enjoy high levels of constitutional or statutory autonomy, and even though boards of governors or trustees stand in an intermediate governing position vis-à-vis the educational institutions themselves. The pattern of decentralization, diversity, and institutional autonomy that has resulted from these arrangements—as well as the distinctive competitive mix of public and private institutions—has been argued by many to be essential to the growth and high quality of American higher education (e.g., Vest 2005). In the context of this distinctive pattern of financing, governance, and autonomy, I point to another fundamental vicious circle that appears to be sapping the vitality and workability of that long-standing pattern.

I mentioned the accountability movement beginning the 1980s and accelerating through the 1990s; one commentator spoke of the rise of the "audit society" (Power 1997). Among the factors that stimulated the movement were pressures to maintain a global competitive edge (Steedle 2010), concerns over the rising costs of education—almost twice as fast as inflation (Long 2010)—and general concerns with performance and accountability in industry and government. The essence of the movement is that "higher education institutions . . . demonstrate that they are meeting their stated educational missions and goals and that the supporting evidence they provide is objectively and continuously gathered and reported" (Hernon and Dugan 2004: xv). Accountability meant ratcheting up the requirements for assessment of performance, reporting by those audited, direct and indirect control by the state and their auditing agents, and loss of institutional autonomy (independence and internal accountability) on the part of publicly audited institutions. It is not often named as such, but increased public accountability is simultaneously a decline of political trust in the targeted institutions (Scott 2001).

The movement for auditing educational institutions was an international one and extended even further in the United Kingdom and Australia than the United States. In keeping with the scientific and bureaucratic mind-set of the auditors, the methodological pressures that accompanied the movement were to *standardize* the process, to *measure* the results of the audit, to present those measures in *quantitative* terms, and thus yield a *precise* account of individual and organizational *performance* on the part of the audited institutions. As an extension of the accountability logic, it was also believed that institutional performance could be *changed* in the direction of efficiency by rewarding institutions financially on the basis of the results of audits.

The auditing movement accelerated in the 1990s (Gaither, Nedwek, and Neal 1994). There was, first, a shift from campus assessment methods to performance measures. Also, numbers of state legislatures took initiatives to establish and implement evaluations based on these measures. By 1992 two-thirds of the states had adopted requirements that universities and colleges report on their performance, and by 1997 some ten states had tied formulae for funding to performance measures (El-Khawas 2005). A great variety of measures was deployed for organizational performance: GRE scores for students, graduation completion rates, time to degree, job placement rate, contributions to states in areas of science and engineering, and student satisfaction (Long 2010). When the methodology was extended to faculty productivity, it included measures such as numbers of various types of publications, citation rates, percentage of authorship, number of grants awarded—all measures, incidentally, that highlighted the quantity of research activity but seldom its quality (see Martin 2010).

Predictably, the application of auditing procedures to institutions of higher education generated as many critics—mainly administrators and faculty—as it did enthusiasts, as well as the identification of as many weaknesses as promises. The major methodological criticisms are these:

- Colleges and universities are institutions with goals that are too general and too multiple in purposes to be able to measure precisely whether goals have been realized. Input–output measures reduce this process to a "mechanistic view" (Neal 1995). Trow put it as follows: "Education is a process pretending to be an outcome. That is what makes all measures of educational outcomes spurious" (Trow 1998: 52).

- Because of this circumstance, it is erroneous to move toward objective, "measurable," quantitative indices of efficiency; to do so is to treat colleges and universities unfairly and to distort the processes that transpire within them.

- Even if differences among institutions are found—for example, differences in graduation rates or test scores—it is impossible to assess whether these result from educational "value added" imparted by the college or university, or from other causes. They may well be the product of high talents that students bring to the institution. This problem of controlling for other variables plagues evaluation research in general.

- Closely related, it is difficult if not possible to infer precise effects from measures taken in naturalistic settings (see Hartnett 1971).

- Institutions of higher education are already subjected to many forms of accountability—to accrediting agencies, to the federal granting agencies and foundations, to regents or trustees, to coordinating councils, and to "consumer guides" that rank them. They also have highly developed internal accountability mechanisms, such as the grading of students, teaching evaluations, and constant appraisal of faculty research productivity (see Seldin and Associates 2006).

- As a result, yet another layer of inadequate evaluation by state agencies is wasteful of time and resources. An extreme critic dismissed the whole accountability enterprise as "rituals of verification" (Power 1997).

If these principled objections are not enough, accountability schemes also typically face rough sledding in their implementation. Administrators continuously oppose and attempt to influence—if not stonewall—them. Many faculty take a position of "active or passive opposition" to institutional evaluation (Lopez 2004: 37). More generally, faculty members—the group that supposedly should be involved in the "accounting" process—are usually insulated from the process by handing the recording and reporting over to college and university bureaucrats. Those bureaucrats, on their part, tend to sift and submit information selectively and present the best face (e.g., on teaching loads and "contact hours"). State bureaucrats, on their part, often routinely file reports and regard the situation as satisfactory if the proper reporting procedures have been followed (see Grizzle 2002).

In practice, state accountability efforts in higher education have had a checkered history. Though diffused and adopted by many states and their educational institutions by the 1990s, the initial responses of many campuses were "often adaptive, ephemeral, and cosmetic" (Gaither 1995). Many practices became routinized, and some were discontinued after a period of time. Programs linking budgetary support to measures of efficiency and productivity have tended to be short-lived (Long 2010: 156). It could be plausibly argued, moreover, that in the end accountability efforts have had unknown or zero impact on the efficiency and productivity of those institutions they were intended to affect (El-Khawas 2004).

I emphasize the accountability phenomenon to underscore a paradox: that at precisely the same time that state legislatures were initiating the annual *decreases* of educational budgets, they were simultaneously taking steps to *increase* the intrusiveness of states in the governance process. One might attempt to resolve this paradox by claiming that states were doing both of these for the same reason: a loss of faith and confidence in the nation's system of higher education and its institutions. Be that as it may, the historical episode reveals a larger, more pervasive paradox or contradiction: as states' responsibility (in the form of public and financial support) has withered and continues to do so—down to levels of 10–15 percent of annual budgets in extreme cases—their governance of these institutions has remained virtually the same or perhaps increased. Someone should invent a slogan that parallels our famous colonial "taxation without representation" battle cry. Perhaps it should be "power without responsibility" or "politics without economics."

In all events, that contradiction has put the higher education system on a collision course that seems destined to reach some breaking-point and, it is hoped, some legal-institutional resolution. The contradiction has already generated a barrage of talk about formal "privatization" to acknowledge the historical trends—and some institutional efforts to achieve privatization de facto, as in Michigan and Virginia—without realizing all the implications of all that that privatization might entail: for example, what is the legal status of the accumulated physical plant and other infrastructure if "privatization" proceeds? The contradiction has raised another serious question: How an institution can simultaneously be public and not really state supported? A third question: Is it viable to retain the existing form of trustee-cum-state governance as a "quo" when the "quid" of support has withered so profoundly? Of all the anomalies and problems I am considering in this chapter, this complex of issues seems to be the most profound in its prospects.

THE MANY FACES OF COMMERCIALIZATION

Looking at the past few decades, there is a dominating theme in the national dialogue about higher education: its commercialization into forms that are increasingly indistinguishable from business enterprises (above, pp. 58–60). That din is loud and incessant, and it has overwhelmed the contemporary critical literature on higher education. In a desperate effort to master and sort out the many threads of this theme, I have fashioned an acronym—GAMMA—that runs as follows:

G: globalization
A: academic capitalism

M: marketization

M: managerialism

A: accountability

Some celebrate these trends as the only things that can save archaic and inefficient institutions, but others fear they are a death knell for academic principles and institutions.

The Language and Imagery of Corporatism and Its Consequences

Some commentators have noted—and usually rued—the invasion of business and managerial language into the administrative life of colleges and universities (e.g., Bok 2003). Sample terms are knowledge industry, cost–benefit analysis, competition, entrepreneurship, efficiency, marketing, outsourcing, organizational reengineering, best practices, strategic choices, and treating incoming students as "inputs," graduates as "outputs," and the intervening process as "throughput." The many business fads that have invaded higher education circles during the past half-century contribute to the parade of corporate language (Birnbaum 2000).

In one sense objections to this language seem minor, because names are not sticks and stones and in and of themselves do not necessarily produce negative consequences. However, insofar as they are symptoms of a new *cultural* outlook, they can divert and weaken if not destroy traditional academic values. It is argued that "if universities were to embrace a commercial ethos then the consequences for the concept or *idea* of the university would be dire" (McCaffery 2010 61). A pragmatic "business" outlook downplays the real "business" of universities and colleges: commitment to the intellectual life, pursuit of knowledge and truths independent of "payoff," and examination, cultivation, and criticism of culture, institutions, and the high ideals of civilization. The language connotes entrepreneurial individualism and erodes the ideal of a community of teaching and inquiring scholars. To extreme critics it means that "universities will turn tricks for anyone with money" (White and Hauck 2000: 30). The business culture does all these things by elevating financial and organizational preoccupations and making the "tending of the shop" the main focus. By contrast, academic

traditionalists often share the inherited view that the university, a funda-
mentally moral and cultural enterprise, should be "above" material concerns (above, pp. 7–8) that corrupt that academic morality.

Student Consumerism

Once upon a time, it is believed, colleges and universities decided what
kind of education is right or good for students and that for students to
learn was both a privilege and a future good. Yet compromises with this
principle began early. One might regard the thread of "vocationalism"
in state institutions in the wake of the Morrill Acts of 1862 and 1890 as,
among other things, gestures in the direction of student future occupational interests. One might also regard Eliot's introduction of the elective
system at Harvard as a consumerist gesture toward students (though
Eliot himself advanced and defended it on academic grounds); it was
certainly attacked vigorously by conservatives in their efforts to retain
the required classical studies and subsequently by activist reformers
such as Woodrow Wilson, Robert Maynard Hutchins, and Alexander
Meikeljohn. Meikeljohn referred to the elective system as "intellectual
agnosticism, a kind of intellectual bankruptcy" (1920: 42). (Note the
moral/religious reference in "agnosticism.") Subsequent movements
toward breadth and student choice, moreover, moved further toward accommodating students; the term "cafeteria" literally suggests the availability of servings of food to be consumed.

Still, however, in the heyday of the power of professional academics (identified by Jencks and Reisman [1968] in the post–World War II
period), student interests appeared to be subordinated to faculty power:

> Academicians today [late 1960s] decide what a student ought to know,
> how he should be taught it, and who can teach it to him. Not only that—
> their standards increasingly determine which students attend their col-
> leges, who feels competent once he arrives, and how much time he has
> for non-academic activities. (Jencks and Reisman 1968: 510)

Yet little more than a decade later Reisman was writing about "an era
of rising student consumerism" (1980). He laid the cause mainly to the

increasing competition for students (which set in during the 1970s with the relative decline of student numbers). Different institutions had different reference points in this competition. Private and public elites competed with institutions of their own kind in the highly talented market; institutions with lesser drawing power competed in the generally shrinking market. This competition constituted an "expansion of student [market] power" (Reisman 1980: xxix). The 1960s had also witnessed a great but in many ways temporary augmentation of student power in direct political protest and activism.

While the combinations of causes are not completely understood, the manifestations of consumerism, or more broadly, catering to students, are the following:

- Advertising their institutions in the media, often promising or intimating a "good life," including partying in the undergraduate years and occupational success thereafter.

- Courting students and their families via the secondary schools and direct personal contact.

- In some cases lowering admission standards and admitting students who cannot compete, do not graduate, and build up indebtedness, hardship, and exploitation through student loans (Collinge 2009)

- The "student aid game" (Kirp 2005), with assertions and some evidence of outright fraudulent behavior.

- Generous perks in housing, eating facilities, and other comforts of life, creating a "coddled class." Superfluous administrative positions—such as "Dietetic Internship Director," and "Vice President of Student Success"—were actually advertised in the *Chronicle of Higher Education* (Hacker and Dreifus 2010: 30).

- Weakening or dismantling requirements in majors and general education programs.

- Grade inflation, a combination of student expectations ("Undergraduates regard good grades as a birthright"—Kirp 2005: 119), faculty spinelessness, and reluctance of institutions to "hold the line" on grading out of apprehension that do so would unduly downgrade student performance, punish them in the job market, and might generate a negative reputation (and reduced student applications) for the institution.

As a rule, "consumerism" is a condemnatory word, suggesting an ill in itself, and likely to reflect a general, knee-jerk evaluation based on antimaterialist sentiments and an unexamined assumption that students should lead a directed, ascetic life after enjoying the privilege of being admitted to college. Logic, however, suggests a more qualified reaction. So long as we have institutionalized a decentralized, quasi-market, competitive situation for students, and so long as failure to secure students runs contrary to institutions' interests, it seems unreal and unfair to blame institutions for behaving as though they are in a market and seeking to survive. Competition for students does not appear to be a wrong in itself; not to compete seems self-defeating. What is reprehensible are the excesses that include demonstrably sacrificing academic standards, making a mockery of evaluation and placement, and exploiting underqualified students by admitting them in order to enhance institutional income from fees available through financial aid and loans (Toby 2010). My preference is that such excesses should be controlled and punished not by external agencies but should be dealt with codes of ethics promulgated by educational associations themselves, with power to expose and publicize bad practices.

A cautionary tale about this preference, however, is found in the history of consumerism in intercollegiate athletics, which informs us about potential pathologies of the market and the difficulties of self-regulation. The urge to win and gain big-time status, stoked by committed (and often paying) alumni, is nearly irresistible. Coaches' salaries and bonuses have spiraled upward. Colleges and universities dream about but only occasionally realize substantial income from some sports. The involvement of the commercial media has reached both dizzying and controlling proportions. In consequence, consumerism in recruiting and indulging athletes has spiraled, especially but not exclusively in the major sports of football and basketball. Recruiting itself is a high art form in persuading, promising, and pressing—and sometimes violating the rules. The competitive provision of athletic training and recreational facilities is nothing short of an arms race. Colleges and universities provide special tutoring and student-athletic programs to help keep athletes from falling into ineligibility, and the search for "gut" courses, soft majors, and silently conspiring, easy-grading professors is a continuing process. The NCAA has developed and exercises sanctions against violators, but the annual flow of violations, both detected and undetected, continues. It is doubtful that competition for students in general will reach such proportions because the commercial temptations to recruit them will never be as high, but the excesses of big-time athletics should stand as an extreme reminder.

(To utter these words might seem to be an embarrassment for me. In the early 1990s I chaired a blue-ribbon commission on intercollegiate athletics at Berkeley, the report of which has been widely interpreted as endorsing big-time intercollegiate athletics on the Berkeley campus [Chancellor's Blue Ribbon Commission on Intercollegiate Athletics 1991]. It is true that we found Cal's pattern of settling for mediocre performance in a major conference to be unsatisfactory and recommended that the campus decide either to take participation in the (then) Pac 10 seriously or revert to a lesser commitment to intercollegiate competition, perhaps on the Ivy League model. But that recommendation was also accompanied by a variety of suggested policies to assure financial and organizational responsibility. And when I personally submitted the report to Chancellor Chang-lin Tien, I suggested, without apparent effect, that he forthwith form another commission on excesses in athletics, having in mind that no matter how high-minded an institution, commitment to the big time also generates big-time temptations.)

Economizing as a Way of Life

Derek Bok lists "efforts to economize in university expenditures" (2003: 3) as one of meanings of "commercialization" in higher education. I hesitate to include a section on this topic, however, because it does not have precisely the same connotations of "commercialism" that the other headings do. Such economizing is typically regarded as the child of necessity—falling revenues and increasing costs—and not so much an expression of a positive market ideology, even though much of the general managerial literature of past decades has rhapsodized about the competitive value of downsizing, outsourcing, reengineering, and the virtues of leanness and meanness (e.g., Shleifer and Vishny 2005).

Economizing includes reducing staff, combining a number of positions into fewer positions, mass purchasing of supplies, removing services and perks such as library delivery services, cutting back purchases (e.g., library subscriptions to marginal scholarly journals), imposing fees for previously gratuitous services such as telephones ("nickeling and diming" to the victims), exhortations for speed-up on the part of employees, and unbundling and outsourcing activities (e.g., regulation of parking) to specialized firms. One special consequence of these measures should be noted: while many modes of economizing have clear economic and administrative rationales, many of them constitute a special kind of "relative deprivation"—removing or charging for things that were previously free or less expensive. They fall in the same category of banks' imposition of service charges on debit cards when those services were originally free. Such economies, even those small in magnitude, are often especially grating and productive of low morale, because they are *symbolic* of a general tightness and meanness and perhaps signify degradations of employees who have professional or quasi-professional expectations. This effect is one of a larger range of consequences that arise when administrative decisions are guided solely by economic or managerial considerations without taking into account important human dimensions (see Smelser and Reed 2012).

A final twist on the economic impulse has to do with the institution of academic tenure, which I will discuss in more general terms later. The topic has become more controversial in the past two decades. One line of attack is a traditional political one—that tenure provides a haven for irresponsible "tenured radicals" who have corrupted the system (Sykes 1988; Anderson 1992). Another line of criticism emanating mainly from economists (e.g, Amacher and Meiners 2004) focuses on the tenure system's economic inefficiencies. Tenure is a rigidity that prevents shifting resources from poor-performing departments to high-performing ones. Tenure protects dead wood because it keeps faculty members on from year to year, without effective sanctions to improve their performance. It is an enormous fixed cost that prevents budgetary flexibility and inhibits "efficient and competitive" strategies. It prevents colleges and universities from adapting rationally to difficult budgetary times. Tenure is an enemy of accountability in that it resists assessing and improving performance. Some call for the end of tenure, maintaining that academic freedom can be preserved without it; more modest proposals call for better and more circumstantial evaluation of faculty, the adoption of mechanisms of post-tenure review (which many universities have adopted in one form or another), and the use of multiyear contractual arrangements, which may or may not be renewed. My own view is that this economic logic has some merit, but that the proper approach to such fundamental institutions as academic tenure cannot be approached on market-efficiency grounds alone. The application of an exclusive economic-managerial approach may be destructive of the recruitment of top talent and may open the door to diminished protection of academic freedom.

University–Industry Relations

Sensitivities about the relations between educational goals of higher education and economic interests find their roots in the embeddedness of education in the spiritual and moral dimensions of life. Expectably, American society, with its strong instrumentalist and materialist threads, has not escaped conflicts expressing these sensitivities. Open political conflicts go back at least one-and-one half centuries. The dramatic act in this drama was the Morrill Acts, which granted federal lands to the states to develop state institutions dedicated to agriculture and commerce. Though variably implemented, the legislation underscored and gave legitimacy to the twin ideas that these institutions would develop selected "service" functions of institutions of higher education and would contribute to the surging national interest in economic development and competitiveness. That emphasis was not without opposition, and in some states fundamental quarrels and conflicts developed over the nature of academic life: traditional cultural emphases or applied knowledge in service of economic interests (e.g., see Douglass 2000). I referred to the Dewey-Veblen-Hutchins assaults in the early nineteenth century on vocationalism, business schools, and domination of corporate interests in higher education, assaults that revealed the same tension between the academic and economic emphases.

The past three decades, dating from the early 1980s, have witnessed a continuing firestorm on this perpetual issue. The interests of commerce and industry have become more paramount in the life of the university, to such an extent that some have proclaimed a complete convergence of interests and structure of the two, a takeover by business interests, and the corruption, even death of academic ideals and practices (see above, pp. 58–59). My reading is that the development is real, though the consequences are selective, not total. In this section I develop a qualified commentary on the recent historical scene.

The critical year was 1980, the passage of the famous Bayh-Dole Act by the United States Congress. While previous political administrations—notably that of Richard Nixon—had made some moves to encourage business–university cooperation, the act of 1980 was a new and decisive event. We remind ourselves that the 1980s were those years of frenzied panic over the apparent decline of American economic competitiveness and the success of other countries, notably Japan and Germany. These governments of these countries, moreover, had not been shy in involving themselves in fostering and encouraging economic projects. The passage of the Bayh-Dole Act was one of the many responses to the larger national and international scenes at the time (above, p. 92).

The law was an intrusion of the government into industry–university relations. Its import was basically legal and permissive: to allow universities to share in income from patented inventions and products that were developed by university scientists and scholars and implemented in various kinds of cooperative enterprises launched by business and universities. That permissiveness, however, constituted a welcome opportunity that came on a scene in which resources had become increasingly problematical. Here is how Bowie described the convergence of forces:

> Whatever qualms Congress had previously had regarding private benefit from the expenditure of public funds were erased by the growing threat of international economic competition and by the perceived decline in research and developmental capacities of American industry. Moreover,

Congress had cut direct government support for basic research. Universities had a double incentive to work cooperatively with industry. (1994: 19)

The situation was a clear instance of resource dependency: various resources for higher education were stagnating or eroding—or threatening to do so—and the pressure to find new, compensating ones was building correspondingly (Slaughter and Leslie 1997). In this environment colleges and universities had already begun to be more aggressive in securing grants and contracts from the private sector, expanding instructional services to businesses, and economizing on hiring practices (Slaughter and Leslie 1997: 100). Finally, there was a further sense of opportunity because so much promising, cutting-edge research—especially in computers and biotechnology—was already being conducted in the academy (Nelkin, Nelson, and Kiernan 1987).

In such an environment the research universities responded eagerly. Many set up machinery to facilitate the registering of patents and to form relationships and alliances with industry. As of 1980, twenty-five universities had technology transfer and licensing offices; by 1990 the figure had grown to two hundred (Cohen et al. 1998: 181–82). Prior to 1980, around 250 patents per year were granted to universities; in 1998 the number was 3,151 (Slaughter and Rhoades 2008).

The development of these diverse activities have displayed a number of expectable—if we look at history—characteristics:

- They have been concentrated in relatively few research institutions. In the 1990s the hundred largest research universities received more than 90 percent of all patents awarded. Recent figures indicated that two-thirds of the monies were generated by thirteen universities (Slaughter and Rhoades 2008: 39–40). This concentration follows the pattern of the "rich getting richer" exhibited in foundation, private-donor, and federal support patterns. The principle is the same: development funds gravitate toward centers of talent and reputation, and these are rewarded disproportionately. Also, collaboration is highly concentrated by field of inquiry; the winners are the sciences (especially bioscientific and medical research), engineering, computer science, and the nation's business schools.

- The benefit–cost picture is clouded by the fact that opportunity seeking creates significant accretions—technology-transfer administrators and staff, legal staff and advisors, public relations officers—even in institutions that are not especially successful in generating income.

- When all is said and done, the actual percentage of higher education's income from the private business sector is relatively small in comparison with other sources—less than 10 percent of university research funding since the 1980s (Vest 2005: 39).

The most profound threat of university–industry collaboration is that it is inimical to higher education's fundamental values. I derive the following list from a statement from Association of American University Professors in 1983, a statement from Stanford University in 1993 (see Bowie 1995), and summary statements by two scholars (Dong 1995; King 2009):

- Conflict of commitment: diversion of intellectual energy, the academic agenda, and research activities. This includes excessive absence of faculty from the campus in consulting and conducting or supervising business-related research. It also involves a loss of academic control over the research agenda.

- Breach of the academic principle of public disclosure of research results in a variety of ways—suppression, distortion, or delay of publication—mainly in the interest of gaining market advantage over competitors. An example is holding back damaging results of clinical trials. The larger effects are to limit freedom of inquiry.

- Limitations on cross-fertilization of research if universities accept confidentiality agreements with corporations.

- Neglect of classroom education.

- Conflict of interest, including securing personal profits from joint university–corporate operations; advertising products for profit in the name of science; selective hiring of company employees or consultants, university students, or staff; and exploitation of employees and assistants for personal gain. Conflict of interest issues also include failure to disclose corporate and financial ties.

- Increased envy or conflict among colleagues; indirect degradation or neglect of nonsupported lines of research activity; further depreciation of the humanities and social sciences, which participate minimally in business–university collaboration by comparison with the sciences and engineering.

These perils differ both in their novelty and their seriousness. Diversion from uninhibited academic pursuits derives from *any* kind of external research opportunities, not just commercial ones. Directions of research are often deflected toward the preoccupations with pressing problems in the larger society, even when funding for their study is not forthcoming. Excessive time away from campus through consulting and advising is a long-enduring problem. Neglect of teaching is a general problem, not exclusively associated with commercial activity. And the downgrading of nonfavored disciplines and areas of inquiry is also a generic problem associated with external research support. All this is to say that we should not ignore the additional, aggravating effects of university–industry collaboration in these problematic areas, but we should not place the entire onus on that activity.

In my estimation, the potentially gravest effects of commercial ties and university research—and those that demand most attention—are two: first, the intensification of the purely *pecuniary* dimension of the accompanying distractions; second, and related, the intensification of the opportunities for conflicts of interest. We have learned about the seriousness of these two from the history of concern with conflicts of interest in the medical profession. We know how tempting opportunities for pecuniary gain can be to professionals of *any* stripe, we know the lengths to which parties will go to deny conflicts of interest and their effects on independent judgments and behavior, we know about the difficulties of regulation, and we know how inventive both professional practitioners and companies (in the medical case the pharmaceutical companies and manufacturers of medical devices) are in crafting new evasions in the face of efforts to regulate. While in my opinion it should fall to the universities and colleges themselves to monitor the complications of academic collaboration with industry, it is also true that they have to be more diligent than they have been in formulating and enforcing conflict-of-interest guidelines and in regulating extracampus involvements.

With respect to the distortions of academic emphasis, we must acknowledge that this is also part of a long-term trend, aggravated by shifts in the direction of commercial collaboration. I agree with critics—though not always with their shrillness—that this long-term trend constitutes a fundamental threat to the idea of the university and collegiate world as a haven of universal and unfettered inquiry into all varieties of research and knowledge. In countering this threat, universities and colleges—and their host societies—will have to deviate from strategies of pure economic opportunism and to reassert their commitments to their institutions and their academic ideals. I know this call may be fanciful, because of the sheer pressure of academic institutions to survive in toughening environments. But fanciful or not, the ultimate results of sacrificing our remarkable institutions of higher learning are a great cost to high civilization.

ONLINE DISTANCE INSTRUCTION AND THE RISE OF THE FOR-PROFITS

The most significant innovation in higher education—as almost everywhere in society—is the computer-led information revolution. Its direct consequences are noticeable:

- It has displaced armies of secretaries and typists employed by individual academics and academic units.

- It has both eased and multiplied scholarly communication among academics, between teachers and students, and between researchers and research assistants.

- It has transformed academic scholarship, mainly in efficient directions—eased scholarly searches, provided vast quantities of research materials online, obliterated the three-by-five card as a research instrument, and streamlined the preparation of materials for publication.

- It has displaced some and threatened much traditional hardcover publishing, raising serious questions about what qualifies as legitimate scientific and scholarly publication relevant to the evaluation and advancement of faculty.

- The last two effects are closely associated with the "library revolution." This is transforming college and university libraries from repositories of published books to be used by scholars to suppliers of Web-based, online materials. They are directly threatened in this latter line of activity by archiving efforts in the private market. In all events their role has become more instructional, "coaching" users in the art of searching in a complex information environment. Some, including Gerhard

Casper, have argued that libraries as physical locations of published materials no longer have any reasons for existing and will disappear over time. Traditional schools of librarianship, which trained conventional librarians, have been transformed one after another into schools of library science, training their students in computer science and its applications to libraries' situations (Darden and Neal 2009).

All of these transformations, momentous as they are, seem to pale when compared to the actual and potential impact of computer technology on much undergraduate and vocational education through computer instruction, called "online courseware" and "distance learning." I dedicate the following remarks to its significance, future, and possible effects—including threats—to established higher education institutions.

The infusions and precise significance of distance learning can best be appreciated by laying out the essentials of traditional course instruction:

- Instruction in gatherings of people in physically constrained spaces—lecture halls, smaller discussion rooms, offices, and less formally in dormitories and coffee shops.

- Opportunity for participation and feedback from students to instructors, often minimal in large lectures but more conspicuous in discussion sections, labs, office hours, and informal conversations outside these settings.

- Evaluation of student performance on exams, papers, and perhaps classroom participation, formal "credits" authorized by faculty, and accumulation of credits into a "degree," granted by and legitimized by a certified educational institution.

- Instruction in interpersonal settings where more informal psychological dynamics unfold—identification with faculty, role modeling, conformity and defiance—and work themselves out in the educational process.

- Often combining instruction with residence—that is, providing living quarters, food, and services to students, though the residential feature is highly variable, ranging from full in many colleges to none in most community colleges.

- Offered for a price that is expressed in tuition and fees, usually not per course but per annum; supplementary courses offered in summer schools or correspondence courses are typically based on a fee-per-course basis.

This package is of long standing, assumed to be the natural state of things for most students and faculty alike, the solid core of educational pedagogy, resistant to change, and typically advertised and defended on grounds of "quality." It has stood the test of time, and some notable episodes, such as the effort in the 1960s to "pipe" televised lectures into supplementary halls, did not gain general currency.

Since the onset of online technology, however, traditional classroom teaching has been partially displaced through the use of computerized instruction that makes variable use of many of the techniques of traditional pedagogy but dissociates concrete space and specific time of delivery from the process by the use of computer technology. The forms are variable, and they can best be understood according to the degrees to which they "unbundle" the ingredients of the traditional model. Though long-distance learning has become a preoccupation of almost all institutions in one way or another, it has become closely associated with profit-making institutions.

The most dramatic and publicly discussed model is the University of Phoenix, with its enrollment moving toward a half-million students and heralding the creation of similar institutions. Its classes are online, its designers of courses and instructors are non-tenure-track, and its clientele is represented by high proportions of "nontraditional" students above the 18–22 age range, ethnic minorities, and women.

More generally, for-profit institutions are predominantly vocational—industry specific, career specific, even job specific (Hentschke, Lechuga, and Tierney 2010); as such, they compete with and have displaced many proprietary institutions. Being for-profit, they are also tax paying and investment attracting. Most are small; as of 2010, they constitute 39 percent of all institutions in higher education, though only 9 percent of enrollments. Teaching loads are heavy, and faculty are scarcely involved in research (Brewer, Gates, and Goldman 2002). Also in 2010, they awarded 15 percent of associate's degrees (mainly the degrees awarded by community colleges), only 4–5 percent of bachelor's degrees (but fastest growing; Hacker and Dreifus 2010: 8), 8 percent of master's degrees, and 3 percent of all doctoral degrees in the United States (Hacker and Dreifus 2010). Enrollments of minority students (black and Hispanic) are conspicuously high (Alfred et al. 2009: 54). As these figures suggest, they are most directly competitive with other proprietary institutions and vocational programs in community colleges, where many students attend part time and work to support themselves (Farrington 1999); less but somewhat competitive with four-year colleges; and scarcely competitive with doctoral and research institutions, except with schools, departments, and programs that are explicitly vocational. For all intents and purposes they do not compete with elite residential institutions that have surpluses of applicants for traditional college degrees—"the University of Phoenix and similar organizations are not likely to put the Ivy League out of business anytime soon" (Farrington 1999: 83). (Those for-profits that offer advanced degrees are potentially competitive with doctoral institutions, but that competition is not salient as yet.)

Two features critical for the success of these for-profit and mainly online institutions are (a) their courses and degrees have been accredited by official agencies, which legitimizes their charging of fees because they offer courses carrying credit, and (b) if students are enrolled in these institutions—being accredited—they become eligible for student grants and loans; these grants amd loans constitute, in effect, a major source of subsidization for the for-profits. Because of this, opportunities arise for fraudulent institutions bent on gain from student aid. So do opportunities for crackdowns on such institutions, as happened with for-profits during the GI Bill era and the correspondence schools in the late 1960s and 1970s (Kinser 2006). Predictably, traditional faculty have taken a dim view of these for-profit institutions, criticizing them for their low quality, for relying on temporary and part-time faculty, for ignoring faculty rights and academic freedom, for neglecting library resources, and for making decisions on financial, not academically appropriate, grounds (Fisher and Koch 2004).

Many four-year colleges and community colleges, while retaining their traditional status, have also established programs and divisions to offer distance-learning credits toward degrees. Examples are the University of Maryland's University College and Penn State's Global Campus, which offer both online and campus instruction, the former bent toward the vocational and professional. In many respects these are technological extensions of long-established correspondence courses, summer schools, evening classes, and other outreach programs (Trow 1997). Because they offer courses for credit and charge fees—even though nonprofit—they can be said to be in direct competition with the nonprofits for students. A major unanswered question is this: Where will the traditional and the for-profits, respectively, ultimately stand with respect to endowing market advantage to their students and, less tangibly, as "credentialing" institutions in the status hierarchy?

Elite private and public institutions have also entered the long-distance learning arena, but on quite different terms (for a general treatment, see Walsh 2011). The 1990s witnessed a diversity of experiments, among the most notable Columbia University's Fathom, a proposed moneymaking operation that failed to attract sufficient customers. Another was the consortium (including Oxford, Princeton, Stanford, and Yale) to offer courses for fees, mainly to alumni. That experiment was also temporary. Since that time, premier universities have taken a different route, such as simply making their college curriculum free online without credit, the most notable of which is MIT's Opencourseware program. Others are the more selective and highly successful Open Learning Initiative of Carnegie Mellon, the also-selective Open Yale Courses, and the more limited webcast.berkeley. These long-distance offerings are free and not-for-credit, thus largely removing these institutions effectively from competition for students with the for-profits and keeping separate and intact the "medallion" imprimatur of their own traditional degree programs. Two problems characterize these efforts at elite institutions. The first is sustainability. Most of the programs have been initiated and sustained early by foundation grants—especially from the Mellon and Hewlett foundations—but given foundation policies, these cannot be expected to be permanent subsidies. The second is contentiousness. Universities' intentions and involvement in distance learning continually confront opposition from faculty, based on arguments that online education debases the "quality" of instruction, as well as more concrete guild-protective considerations including the apprehension that administration of online instruction diminishes faculty control of the curriculum (Kirp 2003).

One of the most frequently identified—but seldom thoroughly analyzed—developments over the past several decades is the spectacular growth of temporary (non-tenure-track) and part-time faculty. Though said to be "invisible" (Gappa and Leslie 1993), investigators have uncovered forty-nine separate names—including adjunct, non-ladder, contingent, subfaculty—by which they are called (Worthen and Berry 1999). The rate of growth in these categories has been astounding. Between 1970 and 2001 part-timers increased by 376 percent, more than five times the rate of full-time faculty; the number of full-time, tenure-track faculty members is now agreed to be below 50 percent of the total (Schuster and Finkelstein 2006). These adjunct faculty supplement the work of another very large class of nonfaculty instructors—graduate student teaching assistants—who are also temporary in that they have semester or year appointments and that they assist for a few years and then leave the institution. The proportions of these categories vary by segment: research, doctoral-granting institutions utilize their own students as teaching assistants and use adjunct faculty least; four-year colleges make more use of adjunct faculty; community colleges even more; and proprietary, for-profit institutions are mainly temporary or part time (Baldwin and Chronister 2002). Distributions of part-time faculty alone show the same results, with the lowest rates in private not-for-profits and highest in for-profits, with public institutions at intermediate points (Kinser 2006).

Variety is name of the game with respect to this adjunct faculty. I will not be concerned with those long-standing and relatively nonproblematic "experts" such as physicians, artists, and businessmen who periodically add their knowledge and talents to an institution's academic program. Nor am I concerned with "career-enders" who teach occasionally after retiring. I refer, rather, to that large number of part-time and temporary (non-tenure-track) faculty that are taken on to meet fluctuations in enrolment demand, to meet unexpected instructional expediencies, and to contend with financial imperatives.

This last class is the fastest growing and most problematical. Their numbers and percentages grow higher as one moves down the hierarchy of institutions, with the greatest numbers teaching in the community colleges. They teach mainly writing, language instruction, mathematics, and large, typically lower-division lecture courses—in a word, in those areas that "regular" faculty have cheerfully surrendered, even though they still frequently insist on authorization and control of curricula. The motives of temporary and part-time faculty are multiple—to experience the gratification of teaching collegiate students, to supplement another primary teaching job, to supplement a spouse's income, to cobble a living by teaching simultaneously in several institutions. ("freeway flyers" or "scholar gypsies"). Many are satisfied with their situation, maintaining connections with institutions and activities they love and at the same time avoiding the stresses associated with the pressures of research and publication. Those in vocational-training instruction (e.g., nursing, business, teaching) are most satisfied; those in the social sciences and humanities least so (Benjamin 1998).

Most explanations of the rapid growth of adjuncts stress evident economic factors. On the demand side adjunct appointees cost less because of their lower salaries; they can be easily dismissed or not reappointed, thus avoiding the hiring institutions' continued commitment until retirement; they are often excluded from institutions' costly benefit and retirement programs; and they are a source of year-to-year flexibility for administrators who must adapt to changes in student demand and funding (Rhoades 1996). In addition, once savings from hiring these less costly personnel are realized, they become an integral part of the cost picture, and reversion to more expensive practices becomes difficult (Jacobs 1998). On the supply side are the "reserve army" of academics not employed in tenure-track positions, candidates who attended graduate school but never completed their Ph.Ds, many people in business and other roles who are willing to affiliate on a part-time basis in specialized courses, and spouses who are often academically qualified but immobile because of community and family ties. (In 2003 white men made up 49.6 percent of full-time faculty and white women 30.7%, while in the same year white men were 44.4 percent of part-time faculty and white women 40.8%; National Center for Education Statistics 2003.)

This line of supply-and-demand analysis, however, leaves out of account what has happened with respect to the other and more traditional source of teaching—the full-time, tenure-track faculty, especially in universities. Over the decades their salaries have risen, partly through the rise of service salaries generally (Archibald and Feldman 2011), and partly through the dynamics of emulation and competition among striving institutions. Their teaching loads have declined, also in part because of competition among institutions willing to reduce them as a bargaining chip. Sabbatical leaves continue as significant drains on active teaching. Many faculty have the capacity to use research funds to "buy out" of teaching. Less formally, the desire of faculty in research institutions to teach graduate courses in favor of undergraduate ones is another source of reduced supply of undergraduate teaching. Most of these effects have occurred as a consequence of past structural accretions that in effect downgraded the traditional teaching role. In a word, the costliness *and* unavailability of traditional teaching has escalated the need for and attractiveness of alternatives. The whole situation aggravates an institutional paradox: continued formal control of curriculum and teaching by regular faculty and increased participation of less valued and less rewarded others. It is also a major ingredient in the recipe for alienation and protest against an entrenched, nonperforming elite (above, pp. 36–37).

As early as 1979, one observer said, "[W]e are witnessing a dramatic but relatively unnoticed structural transformation of higher education: the emergence of a quasi-closed elite at the top and a permanent underprivileged stratum of untouchables at the bottom" (Wilke 1979: xii). And in 1987, a special commission of the University of California system— where temporary and part-time employment was less prevalent than in most other types of institutions—called attention to the issues of quality of teaching the employment of these categories raised, as well as their diminished privileges and citizenship (Task Force on Lower Division Education 1987).

The specific disadvantages accruing to this second-class category have been noticed and cataloged. Lower pay is the most obvious. They also typically man courses that are of lower status and least attractive in the eyes of regular faculty. But there are additional disadvantages:

> [They] experience lack of office space [and reduced or no office hours for students], lack of office telephone, lack of computer access, lack of access to photocopying services, and no support for professional development . . . Additionally, part-time faculty members are assigned to faculty mentors, and administrators do not evaluate their work. Therefore, excellent part-time faculty members receive no recognition and substandard teachers get no direction. . . . part-time faculty more often teach lower-level classes than full-time faculty. As a group, part-time faculty are underpaid, overworked, and frequently feel unappreciated and disrespected. (Hutti et al. 1993: 31)

One can add reduced or no health and retirement benefits, except in places where they have gained them through legislation. The negative implications of many of these disadvantages for the quality of teaching seem self-evident (see Ehrenberg 2011).

Other disadvantages that accompany and underscore second-class citizenship are those of social exclusion. Non-tenure-track and part-time personnel are not members of academic senates or kindred associations, and they thus have a lesser role in shared governance (Chait 2002b). In departments, they are typically nonvoting and often not invited to attend meetings. More informally, they are less likely to be included in social occasions and in informal visiting patterns among faculty.

Most suggestions for reforms and attempts to improve the situation of adjunct faculty call for easing the cited disadvantages and for better incorporation in the participatory life and citizenship of the institutions in which they are now marginalized (see Lyons 2007). One has to be somewhat ambivalent, however, about urging their participation in the departmental and committee life of institutions without correspondingly improved pay, status, and fringe benefits, because their unrewarded participation may, in effect, constitute further exploitation. Most pressures to ameliorate come from faculty unions (Berry 2005) that tend to align themselves *against* institutions on bread-and-butter issues rather than to seek greater inclusion as professionals. In keeping with their status, the part-time and temporary are—when compared to regular faculty—much more likely to unionize, even though their temporariness, dispersion, and geographical mobility are obstacles. The principle is that if people are treated as disadvantaged employees rather than professionals, they are more likely to respond politically as disadvantaged employees.

Another general comment on unionization of academics is in order. The movement emerged in the middle to late 1960s, and by 1973 approximately 10 percent of campuses had some form of union (DeCew 2003). Their spread accelerated in the 1980s with the continuing financial exigencies. The main items on unions' agendas tended to be salary, merit increases, working conditions, and benefits. Their spread was correlated negatively with the prestige of institutions and the corresponding "professional" quality of the faculty, with strongest resistance encountered in the research and doctoral-granting institutions, where many faculty saw a conflict between professional values and oppositional organization (Ladd and Lipset 1973). There were also some apprehensions that organizing and bargaining ultimately constituted a threat to academic tenure (DeCew 2003). Several national organizations—the American Federation of Teachers, the National Educational Association, and the American Association of University Professors—serve as umbrellas with which "locals" are affiliated. These organizations are also ranked, in that order, according to militancy and willingness to define their constituencies as "employees" rather than "professionals" (Hutcheson 2000). Speaking generally, unions have become a major feature of the academic landscape and offer a fundamental alternative to traditional "shared governance." At the same time, they have been underrecognized by scholars, largely, I suspect, because most of those likely to do research on them reside in major, elite research universities where ambivalence toward the labor-union model is strongest.

Implications for Tenure

Some observers have argued that the greatest threat to academic tenure lies *not* in periodic attempts by legislators and others who resent faculty dead wood, radical politics, privileged status, and protection from the realities of the market (Chait 2002a) but rather from alterations in the market for faculty. In 1992, the American Association of University Professors pronounced that part-time faculty "undercuts the tenure system, severs the connection between the control of the curriculum and the faculty who teach it, and diminishes the professional status of all faculty members" (quoted in Rhoades 1996: 138). Similar statements have come from the American Federation of Teachers and the National Educational Association. The threats are a combination of (a) the longer-term processes of atrophy of regular faculty through the market forces I have identified (I see no evidence that any of these forces will lessen, given the enduring economic hardships facing higher education) and (b) stumbling and implicit political coalitions between angry adjunct faculty and economy-minded administrators who will not mind, incidentally, if the power of their most powerful—and often most troublesome—constituency, the regular faculty, diminishes. I am not predicting one-time legislation or some other kind of political stroke to end tenure. The more likely situation will be one of "death by fading" as all the forces I have identified— plus the possible migration of academic researchers to nonacademic settings—take their steady toll.

Excursus on Academic Freedom

This seems an appropriate moment to raise explicitly the issue of academic freedom in higher education, for the following reason. Some commentators assert a direct connection between non-tenure-track and temporary employment and academic freedom; one set cited the complaint that "the continued practice of hiring non-tenure-track instructors will threaten academic freedom and the existence of the tenure system" (Gross and Goldenberg 2009: 8). Another asserted baldly that "[w]ithout tenure, there is no assurance of academic freedom" (Darden and Cloud, 2009: 59). That threat, as noted, is mainly one of erosion, as the proportion of tenured faculty stagnates or drops and the proportion of non-tenure-track faculty balloons. Because tenure is so closely associated with the issue of academic freedom historically, the growth of nonregular faculty is also regarded as a threat to the latter. The logic is as follows: tenure has come to be associated with job protection and job security, and via that association, tenured faculty members cannot be discharged or otherwise punished on account of their political views, activities, or memberships. The logic continues with the assertion that non-tenure-track personnel are more vulnerable to arbitrary termination (because they are renewed positions, not tenured ones) for unpopular views or memberships, under the cloak of budgetary stringency or organizational adjustment.

This line of reasoning is confounded by a number of points of vagueness that should be clarified in order to assess whether a genuine threat to academic freedom is carried by changes in the market status of faculty—and, if so, what kind of threat. Here are the main points:

- Academic freedom as such is primarily a principle that protects faculty from punishment for political or personal reasons. The history of higher education has seen periodic episodes of efforts to violate this principle in response to community, religious, and political pressures, usually from the right wing of the political spectrum. Examples come from the era of McCarthyism and the "patriotic correctness" after 9/11 (Wilson 2008). Internal sources (usually from the left) include the movement for "relevance" of teaching and research in the 1970s (Hook 1971) and the forces emanating from "political correctness" associated with multiculturalism and race/class/gender sensitivities, expressed mainly in efforts to regulate hate speech (Klatt 2003; Kors and Silvergate 1998). The faculty establishment (mainly the American Association of University Professors) and other liberal groups of faculty have constituted the principal opposition against such interventions, especially the external ones. As a rule the internal threats are less public and visible, and they are more likely to be exercised through more informal pressures of public opinion. Of these a leading advocate of academic freedom has observed, "I have an ominous feeling that we have met the enemy and . . . it is we ourselves (O'Neill 2000: 27).

- The extent of activities properly covered by "academic freedom" is variable and uncertain. In their most unequivocal form violations are direct retribution for political memberships, views, and behavior. Does it also cover freedom to teach whatever one wishes in the classroom? To some degree yes, but this principle is compromised by counterpressures against faculty who openly indoctrinate students in a political line. Furthermore, academic departments directly control teaching by designing structured curricula. Does it cover freedom to do whatever research one wishes? To a large degree yes, but the opportunity structures for research (found in selectivity of research-support programs in both government an industry), diverts and compromises complete independence in selection of research topics. Does it cover freedom to engage in political protest on the part of faculty? To some degree yes, but protest using the name of the college or university is legitimately regulated, and, as I have suggested, limited by informal but real expectations of civility on the part of faculty. As a result of these ambiguities, completely consistent application of the principle of academic freedom is difficult.

• Academic freedom does not include absolute claims for security of employment or lifetime employment. The American Association of University Professors and the courts have consistently acknowledged that termination of tenured faculty members is legitimate when academic units are discontinued and for reasons of budgetary stringency. That is the legal reality. In practice, administrators are more reluctant to terminate tenured faculty than temporary faculty (preferring instead to relocate them), largely because temporary contracts end automatically and the burden of proof is on renewal, whereas tenured faculty are automatically renewed unless a deliberate decision not to do so is made. For the same reasons, explicit political reactions against terminating tenured faculty are stronger than those against terminating temporary faculty.

These clarifications make more precise the threats of non-tenure-track and temporary employment to both academic tenure and academic freedom. Academic tenure is threatened, not directly as a practice as such, but via attrition of numbers and ultimate decline in political influence (especially if non-tenure-track personnel organize into unions), and in the concentration of the diminishing numbers of tenured-track faculty in higher-prestige institutions. Non-tenure-track status does not and should not, as such, affect academic freedom. Presumably non-tenure-track teachers are equally protected because of their status as faculty. However, the *opportunity* to smuggle in political and other irrelevant considerations in the case of non-tenure-track employees is greater, because their termination and nonrenewal are more nearly "automatic" from year to year; this can more easily obscure the exercise of political and other nonrelevant considerations for nonrenewal (Gross and Goldenberg 2009: 137).

CODA

In this chapter I have dwelt on what I regard as the most compelling problems and potential crises that face American higher education. I have included these under the headings of starvation, accountability, and governance; student consumerism; the language and imagery of corporatism; economizing as a way of life; university–industry relations; online distance instruction and the rise of the for-profits; and nontenured and part-time faculty.

All of these topics have their own reality but are similar in one respect: every one reveals an economic dimension that is at the core of the problem. It is also true that the problems are differentially experienced by different segments and institutions of higher education. From the standpoint of availability of resources and accountability, different categories of institutions—private research, public research, private colleges, public colleges, community colleges, and for-profits—face different exigencies. Private and public elites face different kinds of competition for students than public colleges, community colleges, and for-profits. Given those differences, they engage in different levels and kinds of consumerism. Federal research funding and university–industry cooperation are concentrated at the top of the status hierarchy of institutions. Temporary and part-time personnel are also distributed unevenly in that hierarchy, and regular faculty, tenure, and academic freedom are best protected at the top levels. Finally, different categories of institutions have pursued different strategies with respect to adoption and use of computer technology in instruction.

The most reasonable prediction for the future is that all these categories of institutions adapt according their own particular circumstances. After all, this is the way that they have consistently coped with or taken advantage of changing circumstances in the past. They will attempt to maximize their apparent opportunities and follow apparent survival strategies. In this context I find myself thinking especially about the strategies of elite institutions, both private and public. They are in a good position simply to sustain their privileged positions and to remain at the top of the heap with respect to quality of students, reputation, and access to different kinds of resources. They are most likely to have their full-time tenure track and its faculty maintained (Ehrenberg 2011: 125). The history of higher education has revealed their advantages in a competitive world. I suspect that they, too, will choose to follow the same opportunistic strategies, to compete with their lesser brethren only when they have to do so, to claim monopoly and shun competition when they can, to maximize their resources, and to protect their privileged positions in the short run.

Yet I wonder if this is individualistic strategy is optimal for the long haul. In raising this question, I return to my initial emphasis on the systemic nature of higher education. The excellence of higher education is clearly dependent on the health of primary and secondary education, and the latter's ill health in recent decades has posed problems for and impaired the efforts of all of higher education. Clearly the health of elite institutions depends on the educational health of other segments. Since the elite institutions are typically more influential—though not always more powerful—than the other segments, it strikes me that one strategy of the elites, along with their necessarily self-serving ones, should be to take leadership and join in common social and political cause with others in the nation's education. Their self-interest, survival, and effectiveness as institutions depend in the long run on the health and work of all of them.

References

Alfred, Richard, Christopher Shults, Ozan Jaquette, and Shelley Strickland. 2009. *Community Colleges on the Horizon: Challenge, Choice, or Abundance.* Lanham, MD: Rowman & Littlefield.

Allen , Mark (ed.). 2002. *The Corporate University Handbook: Designing, Managing, and Growing a Successful Program.* New York: AMACOM.

Altbach, Philip G. 2001. "The American Academic Model in Comparative Perspective" In Philip G. Altbach, Patricia Gumport and D. Bruce Johnstone (eds.), *In Defense of American Higher Education*, 11–37. Baltimore, MD: The Johns Hopkins University Press.

Amacher, Ryan C., and Roger E. Meiners. 2004. *Faulty Towers: Tenure and the Structure of Higher Education.* Oakland, CA: The Independent Institute.

American Council on Education. 2007. *The American College President.* Washington, DC: American Council on Education.

Anderson, Martin. 1992. *Imposters in the Temple: American Intellectuals Are Destroying Our Universities and Cheating Our Students of Their Future.* New York: Simon and Schuster.

Archibald, Robert B., and David H. Feldman. 2011. *Why Does College Cost So Much?* New York: Oxford University Press.

Aronowitz, Stanley. 2000. *The Knowledge Factory: Dismantling the Corporate University and Creating True Higher Learning.* Boston: Beacon Press.

Ashby, Eric. 1974. *Adapting Universities to a Technological Society.* San Francisco, CA: Jossey-Bass.

Association of American Colleges. 1985. *Integrity in the College Curriculum: A Report to the Academic Academic Community.* Washington, DC: Association of American Colleges.

Balderston, Frederick. 1974. *Managing Today's Universities.* San Francisco, CA: Jossey-Bass.

Baldwin, Roger G., and Jay L. Chronister. 2002. "What Happened to the Tenure Track?" In Richard P. Chait (ed.), *The Questions of Tenure,* 125–59. Cambridge, MA: Harvard University Press.

Barr, Margaret J., and George S. McClellan. 2011. *Budgets and Financial Management in Higher Education.* San Francisco, CA: Jossey-Bass.

Barzun, Jacques. 1968. *The American University: How It Runs, Where It Is Going.* New York: Harper and Row.

Bate, Jonathan. 2011. "Finding Public Value." *Oxford Today* 24(1):30–31.

Becher, Tony. 1989. *Academic Tribes and Territories: Intellectual Enquiry and the Cultures of Disciplines.* Buckingham, UK: Open University Press.

Benjamin, Ernst. 1998. "Variation in the Characteristics of Part-Time Faculty by General Fields of Instruction and Research." In David W. Leslie (ed.), *The Growing Use of Part-Time Faculty: Understanding Causes and Effects,* 45–60. San Francisco, CA: Jossey-Bass Publishers.

Bennett, William J. 1984. *To Reclaim a Legacy: Report on the Humanities in Higher Education.* Washington, DC: National Endowment for the Humanities.

Berdahl, Robert M. 2008. "Developed Universities and the Developing World: Opportunities and Obligations." In Luc E. Weber and James J. Duderstadt (eds.), *The Globalization of Higher Education,* 45–53. London: Economica.

Berry, Joe. 2005. *Reclaiming the Ivory Tower: Organizing Adjunct to Change Higher Education.* New York: Monthly Review Press.

Bettinger, Eric P., and Bridget Terry Long. 2007. "Remedial and Developmental Courses." In Stacy Dickert-Conlin and Ross Rubenstein (eds.), *Economic Inequality and Higher Eductation: Access, Persistence, and Success,* 69–100. New York: Russell Sage Foundation.

Bianco-Mathis, Virginia, and Neal Chalofsky (eds.). 1999. *The Full-Time Faculty Handbook.* Thousand Oaks, CA: Sage Publications.

Birnbaum, Robert. 2000. *Management Fads in Higher Education: Where They Come From, What They Do, Why They Fail.* San Francisco, CA: Jossey-Bass Publishers.

Birnbaum, Robert, and Frank Shushok, Jr. 2001. "The 'Crisis' Crisis in Higher Education: Is That a Wolf or a Pussycat at the Academy's Door?" In Philip G. Altbach, Patricia J. Gumport, and D. Bruce Johnstone (eds.), *In Defense of American Higher Education*, 59–84. Baltimore, MD: Johns Hopkins University Press.

Blakemore, Colin. 2011. "Fearful Asymmetry." *Oxford Today* 24(1):32–33.

Bok, Derek. 2003. *Universities in the Marketplace: The Commercialization of Higher Education*. Princeton: Princeton University Press.

Bourdieu, Pierre. 1988. *Homo Academicus*. Translated by Peter Collier. Cambridge: Polity Press.

Bowen, Howard R. 1980. *The Costs of Higher Education*. San Francisco, CA: Jossey-Bass Publishers.

Bowen, William M., and Michael Schwarz. 2005. *The Chief Purposes of Universities: Academic Discourse and the Diversity of Ideas*. Lewiston, ME: The Edwin Mellen Press.

Bowie, Norman E. 1994. *University–Business Partnerships: An Assessment*. Lanham, MD: Roman and Littlefield.

Boyer, Ernest L. 1990. *Scholarship Reconsidered: Priorities of the Professoriate*. Princeton, NJ: Carnegie Foundation for the Advancement of Teaching.

Brewer, Dominic J., Susan M. Gates, and Charles A. Goldman. 2002. *In Pursuit of Prestige: Strategy and Competition in US Higher Education*. New Brunswick, NJ: Transaction Publishers.

Brint, Steven. 2011. "The Educational Lottery." *Los Angeles Review of Books* (November 15):1–15.

Brint, Steven, and Jerome Karabel. 1989. *The Diverted Dream: Community Colleges and the Promise of Educational Opportunity in America, 1900–1985*. New York: Oxford University Press.

Brubacher, John S. 1978. *On the Philosophy of Higher Education*. San Francisco, CA: Jossey-Bass Publishers.

Burke, Joseph J. 1999. "Multicampus Systems: The Challenge of the Nineties." In Gerald H. Gaither (ed.), *The Multicampus System: Perspectives on Practice and Prospects*, 40–79. Sterling, VA: Stylus.

Canby, Henry Seidel. 1936. *Alma Mater: The Gothic Age of the American College*. New York: Farrar, Straus, and Giroux.

Chait, Richard P. 2002a. "Why Tenure? Why Now?" In Richard P. Chait (ed.), *The Questions of Tenure*, 7–31. Cambridge, MA: Harvard University Press.

———. 2002b. "Does Faculty Governance Differ at Colleges with Tenure and Colleges without Tenure?" In Richard P. Chait (ed.), *The Questions of Tenure*, 69–100. Cambridge, MA: Harvard University Press.

Chancellor's Blue Ribbon Commission on Intercollegiate Athletics. 1991. "Intercollegiate Athletics at Berkeley." Berkeley, CA: University of California, Berkley.

Cheit, Earl F. 1971. *The New Depression in Higher Education: A Study of Financial Conditions at 41 Colleges and Universities.* New York: McGraw-Hill.

Cheit, Earl F. 1985. "Business Schools and Their Critics," Business and Public Policy Working Paper #BBP-5, Working Papers, University of California Business School. Berkeley, CA: Regents of the University of California.

Christensen, Clayton, Michael B. Horn, and Curtis W. Johnson. 2011. *Disrupting Class: How Disruptive Innovation Will Change the Way the World Learns.* New York: McGraw-Hill.

Cohen, Linda, and Roger G. Noll. 1998. "Universities, Constituencies, and the Role of the States." In Roger G. Noll (ed.), *Challenges to Research Universities,* 31–62. Washington, DC: Brookins Institution Press.

Cohen, Wesley M., Richard Florida, Lucien Randazzese, and John Walsh. 1998. "Industry and the Academy: Uneasy Partners in the Cause of Technological Advance." In Roger G. Noll (ed.), *Challenges to Research Universities,* 171–99. Washington, DC: Brookings Institution Press, 1998.

Collinge, Alan. 2009.*The Student Loan Scam: The Most Oppressive Debt in U.S. History—and How We Can Fight Back.* Boston: Beacon Press.

Cuban, Larry. 1999. *How Scholars Trumped Teachers: Change Without Reform in University Curriculum, Teaching, and Research, 1890–1990.* New York: Teachers College Press.

Darden, Mary Landon, and Robert B. Cloud. 2009. "Future Legal Issues." In Mary Landon Dardon, *Beyond 2020: Envisioning the Future of Universities in America,* 47–62. Lanham, MD: Rowman and Littlefield.

Darden, Mary Landon, and James J. Duderstadt. 2009. "Overview of the Future University Beyond 2020." In Mary Landon Dardon, *Beyond 2020: Envisioning the Future of Universities in America,* 1–12. Lanham, MD: Rowman and Littlefield.

Darden, Mary Landon, and James G. Neal. 2009. "University Libraries of the Future." In Mary Landon Dardon, *Beyond 2020: Envisioning the Future of Universities in America,* 113–21. Lanham, MD: Rowman and Littlefield.

D'Augelli, Anthony R. 1991. "Teaching Lesbian and Gay Development: A Pedagogy of the Oppressed." In William G, Tierney (ed.), *Culture and Ideology in Higher Education: Advancing a Critical Agenda,* 213–33. New York: Praeger.

DeCew, Judith Wagner. 2003. *Unionization in the Academy: Visions and Realities.* Lanham, MD: Rowman and Littlefield Publishers.

Donague, Frank. 2008. *The Last Professors: the Corporate University and the Fate of the Humanities.* New York: Fordham University Press.

Dong, Nelson G. 1995. "University-Industry Symbiosis: The Passing of an Era?" BIOTECH '95. San Francisco, CA: American Law Institute/American Bar Association.

Douglass, John Aubrey. 2000. *The California Idea and American Higher Education: 1850 to the 1960 Master Plan.* Stanford: Stanford University Press.

Duderstadt, James J. 2000. *A University for the 21st Century.* Ann Arbor: University of Michigan Press.

Durkheim, Émile. [1893] 1997. *The Division of Labor in Society.* With an Introduction by Lewis A. Coser, translated by W.{ths}D. Halls. New York: The Free Press.

Ehrenberg, Ronald G. 2011. "Rethinking the Professoriate." In Ben Wildawsky, Andrew P. Kelly, and Kevin Carey (eds.), *Reinventing Higher Education: The Promise of Innovation,* 101–28. Cambridge, MA: Harvard University Press.

El-Khawas, Elaine. 2005. "The Push for Accountability: Policy Influences and Actors in American Higher Education." In Ase Gornitzka, Maurice Kogan, and Alberto Amaral, *Reform and Change in Higher Education: Analyzing Policy Implementation,* 287–303. Dordrecht, The Netherlands: Springer.

Engell, James, and Anthony Dangerfield. 2005. *Saving Higher Education in the Age of Money.* Charlottesville, VA: University of Virginia Press.

Farrington, Gregory C. 1999. "The New Technologies and the Future of Residential Undergraduate Education." In Richard N. Katz and Associates (eds.), *Dancing with the Devil: Information Technology and the New Competition in Higher Education,* 73–94. San Francisco, CA: Jossey-Bass Publishers.

Fecher, R.{ths}J. (ed.). 1985. *Applying Corporate Management Strategies.* San Francisco, CA: Jossey-Bass Publishers.

Fisher, James L. 1989. "Establishing a Successful Fund-Raising Program." In James L. Fisher and Gary H. Quehl, *The President and Fund Raising,* 3–17. New York: Macmillan Publishing Company, 1989.

Fisher, James L., and James V. Koch. 2004. *The Entrepreneurial College President.* Westport, CT: Praeger Publishers.

Fisher, Shirley. 1994. *Stress in Academic Life: The Mental Assembly Line.* Buckingham, UK: The Society for Research into Higher Education and the Open University Press.

Flawn, Peter T. 1990. *A Primer for University Presidents: Managing the Modern University.* Austin, TX: University of Texas Press.

Gaither, Gerald H. 1995. "Editor's Notes." In Gerald H. Gaither (ed.), *Assessing Performance in an Age of Accountability,* 1–3. San Francisco, CA: Jossey-Bass Publishers.

———. 1999. "Preface." In Gerald H. Gaither (ed.), *The Multicampus System: Perspectives on Practice and Prospects,* xviii–xxvi. Sterling, VA: Stylus.

Gaither, Gerald, Brian P. Nedwek, and John E. Neal. 1994. *Measuring Up: The Promises and Pitfalls of Performance Indicators in Higher Education.* Washington, DC: Graduate School of Education and Human Development, the George Washington University.

Gappa, Judith M., and David W. Leslie. 1993. *The Invisible Faculty: Improving the Status of Part-Timers in Higher Education.* San Francisco, CA: Jossey-Bass Publishers.

Geiger, Roger L. 1986. *To Advance Knowledge: The Growth of American Research Universities, 1900–1940.* New York: Oxford University Press.

———. 2004. *Knowledge and Money: Research Universities and the Paradox of the Marketplace.* Stanford: Stanford University Press.

Ginsburg, Benjamin. 2011. *The Fall of the Faculty: The Rise of the All-Administrative University and Why it Matters.* New York: Oxford University Press.

Giroux, Henry A. 2007. *The University in Chains: Confronting the Military-Industrial Complex.* Boulder, CO: Paradigm Publishers.

Gmelch, Walter H., and Val D. Miskin. 1995. *Chairing an Academic Department.* Thousand Oaks, C: Sage Publications.

Gregorian, Vartan, and James Martin. 2004. "Presidents Who Leave, Presidents Who Stay: A Conversation with Vartan Gregorian." In James Martin, James El Samels & Associates, *Presidential Transition in Higher Education: Managing Leadership Change,* 21–28. Baltimore, MD: The Johns Hopkins University Press.

Griffith, Marlene, and Ann Connor. 1994. *Democracy's Open Door: The Community College in America's Future.* Portsmouth, NH: Boynton/Cook Publishers.

Grizzle, Gloria. 2002. "Performance Measurement and Dysfunction: The Dark Side of Quantifying Work." *Public Performance and Management Review* 25:363–69.

Gross, John G., and Edie N. Goldenberg. 2009. *Off-Track Profs: Non-Tenured Teachers in Higher Education.* Cambridge, MA: The MIT Press.

Gumport, Patricia. 1991. "The Research Imperative." In William G. Tierney (ed.), *Culture and Ideology in Higher Educaiton: Advancing a Critical Agenda,* 87–105. New York: Praeger.

Hacker, Andrew, and Claudia Dreifus. 2010 *Higher Education? How Colleges Are Wasting our Money and Failing Our Kids—and What We Can Do About It.* New York: Henry Holt and Company.

Hartnett, Rodney T. 1971. *Accountability in Higher Education: A Consideration of the Problems of Assessing College Impacts.* Princeton, NJ: Educational Testing Service.

Hayes, Dennis, and Robin Wynyard (eds.). 2002. *The McDonaldization of Higher Education.* Westport, CT: Bergin & Garvey.

Hearn, Thomas K. 2006. "Leadership and Teaching in the American University." In David Brown (ed.), *University Presidents as Moral Leaders,* 159–76. Westport, CN: Praeger Publishers.

Hentschke, Guilbert C., Vicent M. Lechuga, and William G. Tierney (eds.). 2010. *For-Profit Colleges and Universities: Their Markets, Regulation, Performance, and Place in Higher Education.* Sterling, VA: Stylus Publishing.

Hernon, Peter, and Robert E. Dugan. 2004. "Preface." In Peter Hernon and Robert E. Dugan (eds.), *Outcomes Assessment in Higher Education*, xv–xvii. Westport, CT: Libraries Unlimited.

Hook, Sidney. 1971. "The Long View." In Sidney Hook (ed.), *In Defense of Academic Freedom*, 11–20. New York: Pegasus.

Hughes, R.{ths}M. 1925. *A Study of the Graduate Schools of America*. Oxford, OH: Miami University Press.

Hutcheson, Philo A. 2000. *A Professional Professoriae: Unionization, Bureaucratization, and the AAUP*. Nashville, TN: The Vanderbilt University Press.

Hutchins, Robert Maynard. 1936. *The Higher Learning in America*. New Haven: Yale University Press.

Hutti, Marianne, Gale S. Rhodes, Joni Allison, and Evelyn Lauterbach. 1993. "The Part-Time Faculty Institute: Strategically Designed and Continually Assessed." In Judith Gappa and David Leslie (eds.), *The Invisible Faculty: Improving the Status of Part-timers in Higher Education*, 31–48. San Francisco: Jossey-Bass Publishers.

Jacobs, Frederic. 1998. "Using Part-time Faculty More Effectively." In David W. Leslie (ed.), *The Growing Use of Part-Time Faculty: Understanding Causes and Effects*, 9–18. San Francisco, CA: Jossey Bass Publishers.

Jencks, Christopher, and David Reisman. 1968. *The Academic Revolution*. Garden City, NY: Doubleday.

Johnstone, D. Bruce. 1999. "Management and Leadership Challenges of Multicampus Systems." In Gerald H. Gaither (ed.), *The Multicampus System: Perspectives on Practice and Prospects*, 3–20. Sterling, VA: Stylus Publishers.

———. 2001. "Higher Education and Those 'Out-of-Control Costs.'" In Philip G. Altbach, Patricia Gumport, and D. Bruce Johnstone (eds.), *In Defense of Higher Education*, 144–65. Baltimore, MD: The Johns Hopkins University Press.

Kamenetz, Anya. 2010. *DIY U: Edupunks, Edupreneurs, and the Coming Transformation of Higher Education.* White River Junction, NH: Chelsea Green Publishing.

Kauffman, Joseph F. 1993. "Supporting the President and Assessing the Presidency." In Richard T. Ingram and Associates, *Governing Public Colleges and Universities: A Handbook for Trustees, Chief Executives, and Other Campus Leaders*, 126–46. San Franciscco, CA: Jossey-Bass Publishers.

Kay, John. 2000. "So We Agree Not to Agree?" *Times Higher Education Supplement* (November 24).

Keller, George. 1983. *Academic Strategy: The Management Revolution in American Higher Education*. Baltimore: The Johns Hopkins University Press.

Kemperer, Ken. 1991. "Understanding Cultural Conflict." In William G, Tierney (ed.), *Culture and Ideology in Higher Education: Advancing a Critical Agenda*, 129–50. New York: Praeger.

Kerr, Clark. 1963. *The Uses of the University.* Cambridge: MA: Harvard University Press.

———. 2001. *Academic Triumphs,* Vol. 1 of *The Gold and the Blue: A Personal Memoir of the University of California, 1949–1967.* Berkeley, CA: University of California Press.

———. 2003. *Political Turmoil,* Vol. 2 of *The Gold and the Blue: A Personal Memoir of the University of California, 1949–1967.* Berkeley, CA: University of California Press.

Kimball, Bruce A. 2009. *The Inception of Modern Professional Education: C.{ths} C. Langdell, 1926–1906.* Chapel Hill, NC: The University of North Carolina Press.

King, C. Judson. 2009. "University Roles in Technological Innovation in California." In John Audrey Douglass, C. Judson King, and Irwin Feller (eds.), *Globalization's Muse: Universities and Higher Education Systems in a Changing World,* 279–98. Berkeley, CA: Berkeley Public Policy Press.

Kinser, Kevin. 2006. *From Main Street to Wall Street: The Transformation of For-Profit Higher Education.* ASHE Higher Education Report, Vol. 31, No. 5. Hoboken, NJ: Wiley Periodicals, Inc.

Kirp, David L. 2003. *Shakespeare, Einstein, and the Bottom Line: The Marketing of Higher Education.* Cambridge, MA: Harvard University Press.

———. 2005. "This Little Student Went to Market." In Richard H. Hersh and John Merrow (eds.), *Declining by Degrees: Higher Education at Risk,* 113–29. New York: Palgrave McMillan.

Kirwan, William E. 2006. "The Morality of Shared Responsibility: Preserving Quality through Program Elimination." In David Brown (ed.), *University Presidents as Moral Leaders,* 147–55. Westport, CN: Praeger Publishers.

Klatt, Heinz-Joachim. 2003. "Political Correctness as an Academic Discipline." *Academic Questions* 16:36–45.

Kors, Alan Charles, and Harvey A. Silvergate. 1998. *The Shadow University: The Betrayal of Liberty on America's Campuses.* New York: The Free Press.

Ladd, Everett Carl, Jr., and Seymour Martin Lipset. 1973. *Professors, Unions, and American Higher Education.* Berkeley, CA: Carnegie Foundation for the Advancement of Teaching and the Carnegie Commission on Higher Education.

Langenberg, Donald N. 1999. "On the Horizon: The Learning System." In Gerald L. Gaither (ed.), *The Multicampus System: Perspectives on Practice and Projects,* 215–30. Sterling, VA: Stylus Publishers, 1999.

Lawrence, G. Ben, and Allan L. Service (eds.). 1977. *Quantitative Approaches to Higher Education Management. Washington,* D.C.: American Association for Higher Education.

Layzell, Daniel T., and Kent Caruthers. 1999. "Budget and Budget-Related Policy Issues for Multicampus Systems." In Gerald L. Gaither (ed.), *The*

Multicampus System: Perspectives on Practice and Projects, 110–27. Sterline, VA: Stylus Publishers.

Long, Bridget Terry. 2010. "Higher-Education Finance and Accountability." In Kevin Carey and Mark Schneider (eds.), *Accounting in American Higher Education*, 141–63. New York: Palgrave-Macmillan.

Lopez, Cecelia L. 2004. "A Decade of Assessing Student Learning: What We Have Learned, and What is Next?" In Peter Hernon and Robert E. Dugan (eds.), *Outcomes Assessment in Higher Education*, 29–71. Westport, CT: Libraries Unlimited.

Lyell, Katherine. 2009. "Market-driven Trends in the Financing of Higher Education: What Can We Learn from Each Other?" In John Aubrey Douglass, C. Judson King, and Irwin Feller (eds.), *Globalization's Muse: Universities and Higher Education Systems in a Changing World*, 81–91. Berkeley, CA: Berkeley Public Policy Press.

Lyons, Richard E. 2007. *Best Practices for Supporting Adjunct Faculty*. Boston, MA: Anker Publishing Company.

Marcus, Jon. 2011. "Old School: Four Hundred Years of Resistance to Change." In Ben Wildawsky, Andew P. Kelley and Kevin Carey (eds.), *Reinventing Higher Education: The Promise of Innovation*, 41–72. Cambridge, MA: Harvard University Press.

Martin, Lawrence B. 2010. "Faculty Scholarly Productivity at American Research Universities," in Kevin Carey and Mark Schneider (eds.), *Accountability in American Higher Education*, 33–119. New York: Palgrave-Macmillan.

McCaffery, Peter. 2010. *The Higher Education Manager's Handbook: Effective Leadership in Universities and Colleges* (second edition). New York: Routledge.

McManis, F.{ths}L. and W.{ths}D. Parker. 1978. *Implementing Management Information Systems in Colleges and Universities*. Littleton, CO: Ireland Educational Corporations.

McMillen, William. 2010. *From Campus to Capitol: The Role of Government Relation in Education*. Baltimore, MD: The Johns Hopkins University Press.

Meikeljohn, Alexander. 1920. *The Liberal College*. Boston: Marshall Jones Company.

Moore, Wilbert E., and Melvin M. Tumin. 1949. "Some Social Functions of Ignorance." *American Sociological Review* 14:787–95.

National Center for Education Statistics. 2003. Table 264, "Full-Time and Part-Time Faculty Instructional Staff in Degree-Granting Institutions, by Race-Ethnicity, Sex, and Selected Characteristics. NCES, 2003.

National Institute of Education. 1984. *Involvement in Learning: Realizing the Potential of American Higher Education*. Washington, DC: National Institute of Education.

Neal, John E. 1995. "Overview of Policy and Practice: Differences and Similarities in Developing Higher Education Accountability." In Gerald H. Gaither (ed.), *Assessing Performance in an Age of Accountability*, 5–10. San Francisco, CA: Jossey-Bass Publishers.

Nelkin, Dorothy, Richard Nelson, and Casey Kiernan. 1987. "Commentary: University-Industry Alliances." *Science, Technology, and Human Values* 21(2):65–74.

Nelson, Stephen. 2007. *Leaders in the Labyrinth: College Presidents and the Battle-ground of Creeds and Convictions*. Westport, CT: Praeger.

Nisbet, Robert. 1971. *The Degradation of the Academic Dogma: the University in America, 1945–1970*. New York: Basic Books.

Nussbaum, Martha. 2011. "Not for Profit." *Oxford Today* 24(1):28–29.

Ogburn, William F., and Meyer F. Nimkoff. 1955. *Technology and the Changing Family*. Boston: Houghton Mifflin.

O'Neill, Robert M. 2000. "Academic Freedom in Retrospect and Prospect." In Peggie J. Hollingsworth (ed.), *Unfettered Expression: Freedom in American Intellectual Life*, 19–30. Ann Arbor, MI: The University of Michigan Press.

Ostriker, Jeremiah P., and Charlott V. Kuh (eds.). 2003. Assisted by James A. Voytuk. *Assessing Research-Doctorate Programs: A Methodological Study*. Washington, DC: The National Academies Press.

Padilla, Arthur. 2004. "Passing the Baton: Leadership Transition and the Tenure of Presidents." In James Martin, James El Samels & Associates, *Presidential Transition in Higher Education: Managing Leadership Change*, 37–58. Baltimore, MD: The Johns Hopkins University Press.

Paradeise, Catherine, and Jean-Claude Thoenig. 2011. "The Road to World Class University: Elites and Wannabes." Paper delivered at "Bringing Public Organizations Back In" conference, Organizational Studies Workshop, at Les Vaux de Cerney, May 25–27.

Parsons, Talcott. 1973. "Epilogue: The University 'Bundle': A Study of the Balance between Differentiation and Integration." In Neil J. Smelser and Gabriel Almond (eds.), *Public Higher Education in California*, 275–99. Berkeley, CA: University of California Press.

Pfeffer, Jeffrey, and G.{ths}R. Slancik. 1974. "Organization Decision Making as a Political Process: The Case of a University Budget." *Administrative Science Quarterly* 19:135–51.

Potter, David, and Arthur W. Chickering. 1991. "The 21st Century: The Role of Government." In Ronald R. Sims and Serbrenia J. Sims (eds.), *Managing Institutions of Higher Education into the 21st Century*, 10–30. New York: Greenwood Press.

Power, Michael. 1997. *The Audit Society: Rituals of Verification*. Oxford: Oxford University Press.

Readings, Bill. 1996. *The University in Ruins*. Cambridge, MA: Harvard University Press.

Reisman, David. 1980. *On Higher Education: the Academic Enterprise in an Era of Rising Student Consumerism.* New Brunswick, NJ: Transaction Publishers.

Rhoades, Gary. 1996. "Organizing the Faculty Workforce for Flexibility." *Journal of Higher Education* 66:629–59.

———. 1998. *Managed Professionals: Unionized Faculty and Restructuring Academic Labor.* Albany, NY: State University of New York Press.

Richardson, Richard C. Jr., and Alicia D. Hurley. 2005. "From Low Income and Minority Access to Middle Income Affordability: A Case Study of the U.S. Federal Role in Providing Access to Higher Education." In Ase Gornitzka, Maurice Kogan, and Alberto Amaral (eds.), *Reform and Change in Higher Education: Analysing Policy Implementation.* Dordrecht, The Netherlands: Springer.

Rosenstone, Steven J. 2005. "Challenges Facing Higher Education in America: Lessons and Opportunities." In Frank Iacobucci and Corolyn Tuohy, *Taking Public Universities Seriously,* 55–86. Totonto: Toronto University Press.

Rosenzweig, Robert M. 1998. *The Political University: Policy, Politics, and Presidential Leadership in the American Research University.* Baltimore, MD: The Johns Hopkins University Press.

Rosovsky, Henry. 1990. *The University: An Owner's Manual.* New York: W.{ths} W. Norton.

Rossi, Peter H., and Howard E. Freeman. 1992. *Evaluation: A Systematic Approach.* Newbury Park, CA: Sage Publications.

Rourke, Francis, and Glenn Brooks. 1966. *The Managerial Revolution in Higher Education.* Baltimore, MD: The Johns Hopkins University Press.

Ruben, Julie A. 1996. *The Making of the Modern University: Intellectual Transformation and the Marginalization of Morality.* Chicago, IL: University of Chicago Press.

Sadovnik, Alan R. 1994. *Equity and Excellence in Higher Education: The Decline of a Liberal Educational Reform.* New York: Peter Lang.

Scarlett, Mel. 2004. *The Great Ripoff in American Education: Undergrads Underserved.* Amherst, NY: Prometheus Books.

Schumpeter, Joseph A. 1934. *The Theory of Economic Development: An Inquiry into Profits, Capital, Credit, Interest, and the Business Cycle.* Cambridge, MA: Harvard University Press.

Schuster, Jack H., and Martin J. Finkelstein. 2006. *The Restructuring of Academic Work and Careers.* Baltimore, MD: The Johns Hopkins University Press.

Scott, Peter. 2001. "Universities as Organizations and Their Governance." In Werner Z. Hirsch and Luc E. Weber (eds.), *Governance in Higher Education: The University in a State of Flux,* 125–42. London: Economica.

Seldin, Peter, and Associates. 2006. *Evaluating Faculty Performance: A Practical Guide to Assessing Teaching, Research, and Service.* Boston, MA: Anker Publishing Company.

Shavit, Yossi, Richard Arum, and Adam Gamoran (eds.). 2007. With Gila Menahem. *Stratification in Higher Education: A Comparative Study*. Stanford: Stanford University Press.

Shleifer, Andrei, and Robert W. Vishny. 2005. "Stock Market Driven Acquisitions." In John J. McConnell and David J. Denis (eds.), *Corporate Restructuring*, 81–97. Cheltenham, UK: Edward Elgar Publishing.

Simon, Herbert A. 2001. "Rationality in Society." In Neil J. Smelser and Paul B. Baltes (eds.), *International Encyclopedia of the Social and Behavioral Sciences*, Vol. 19, 12782–86. Oxford: Elsevier.

Slaughter, Sheila. 1991. "The 'Official' Ideology of Higher Education: Ironies and Inconsistencies." In William G. Tierney (ed.), *Culture and Ideology in Higher Education: Advancing a Critical Agenda*, 59–85. New York: Praeger.

Slaughter, Sheila, and Larry L. Leslie. 1997. *Academic Capitalism: Politics, Policies and the Entrepreneurial University*. Baltimore, MD: The Johns Hopkins, University Press.

Slaughter, Sheila, and Gary Rhoades. 2008. "The Academic Capitalist Knowledge/Learning Regime." In Adrienne S. Chan and Donald Fisher (eds.), *The Exchange University: The Corporatization of Academic Culture*, 19–48. Vancouver, BC: UBC Press.

Smelser, Neil J. 1974. "Growth, Structural Change, and Conflict in California Public Higher Education, 1950." In Neil J. Smelser and Gabriel Almond (eds.), *Public Higher Education in California*, 9–141. Berkeley, CA: University of California Press.

———. 2001. "Foreword." In Clark Kerr, *Academic Triumphs*, Vol. 1, *The Gold and the Blue: A Personal Memoir of the University of California, 1949–1967*, xxix–xxvii. Berkeley, CA: University of California Press.

———. 2010. *Reflections on the University of California: From the Free Speech Movement to the Global University*. Berkeley, CA: University of California Press.

Smelser, Neil J., and John S. Reed. 2012. *Usable Social Science*. Berkeley, CA: University of California Press.

Stadtman, Verne A. 1980. *Academic Adaptations: Higher Education Prepares for the 1980s and 1990s*. San Francisco, CA: Jossey-Bass Publishers.

Steedle, Jeffrey. 2010. "On the Foundations of Standardized Assessment of College Outcomes and Estimating Value Added." In Keven Crey and Mark Schneider (eds.) *Accounting in American Higher Education*, 7–31. New York: Palgrave-Macmillan.

Stokes, Peter. 2011. "What Online Learning Can Teach Us about Higher Education." In Ben Wildawsky, Andre P. Kelley, and Kevin Kelly (eds.), *Reinventing Education: The Promise of Innovation*, 197–224. Cambridge, MA: Harvard University Press.

Streeter, Thomas. 2004. "Romanticism in Business Culture: The Internet, the 1990s, and the Origins of Irrational Exuberance," in Andrew Calabrese and Colin Sparks (eds.), *Toward a Political Economy of Culture: Capitalism and Communication in the Twenty-First Century*, 286–306. Lanham, MD: Rowman and Littlefield Publishers.

Swing, Randy L. 2009. "Higher Education Counts: Data for Decision Support." In Gary L. Olson and John W. Presley (eds.), *The Future of Higher Education: Perspectives from America's Academic Leaders*, 139–47. Boulder, CO: Paradigm Press.

Sykes, Charles J. 1988. *Profscam: Professors and the Demise of Higher Education*. Washington, DC: Regnery Gateway, 1988.

Task Force on Lower Division on Education. 1987. *Lower Division Education in the University of California. A* Report of the Task Force on Lower Division Education. University of California.

Thelin, John R. 2004a. *A History of American Higher Education*. Baltimore, MD: The Johns Hopkins University Press.

——. 2004b. "Higher Education and the Public Trough," in Edward P. St. John and Michael D. Parsons (eds.), *Public Funding of Higher Education: Changing Contexts and New Rationales*, 28–38. Baltimore: The Johns Hopkins University Press.

Toby, Jackson. 2010. *The Lowering of Higher Education in America: Why Financial Aid Should be Based on Student Performance*. Santa Barbara, CA: Praeger.

Touraine, Alain [1974] 1997. *The Academic System in American Society* (with a new Introduction by Clark Kerr). New Brunswick, NJ: Transaction Publishers.

Trani, Eugene P., and Robert D. Holsworth. 2010. *The Indispensable University: Higher Education, Economic Development, and the Knowledge Economy*. Lanham, MD: Roman and Littlefield Publishers.

Trow, Martin. 1990. "The University Presidency: Comparative Reflections on Leadership." In Board of Trustees of the University of Illinois, *Values, Leadership and Quality: The Administration of Higher Education*, 95–119. Urbana, IL: University of Illinois Press.

——. 1997. "The Development of Information Technology in American Higher Education." *Daedalus* 126:293–314.

——. 1998. "On the Accountability of Higher Education in the United States." In William G. Bowen and Harold T. Shapiro, *Universities and Their Leadership*, 15–61. Princeton: Princeton University Press.

Tuchman, Gaye. 2009. *Wannabe U: Inside the Corporate University*. Chicago: University of Chicago Press.

Tussman, Joseph T. 1997. *The Beleaguered College: Essays on Educational Reform*. Berkeley, CA: Institute of Governmental Studies Press.

U.S. News and World Report. 2011. *Ultimate College Guide*. Naperville. IL: Sourcebooks Inc.

Veblen, Thorstein. [1918] 1968. *Higher Learning in America*. New York: Hill and Wong.

Vest, Charles M. 2005. *The American Research University from World War II to the World Wide Web: Governments, the Private Sector, and the Rise of the Meta-University*. Berkeley, CA: University of California Press.

Veysey, Laurence R. 1965. *The Emergence of the American University*. Chicago: University of Chicago Press.

Vogel, Ezra F. 1979. *Japan as Number One: Lessons for America*. Cambridge, MA: Harvard University Press.

Wadsworth, Deborah. 2005. "Ready or Not? Where the Public Stands on Higher Education Reform." In Richard H. Hersch and John Merrow (eds.), *Declining by Degrees: Higher Education at Risk*, 23–38. New York: Palgrave Macmillan.

Walsh, Taylor. 2011. *Unlocking the Gates: How and Why Leading Universities Are Opening Up Access to Their Courses*. Princeton: Princeton University Press.

Washburn, Jennifer. 2005. *University, Inc.: The Corporate Corruption of Higher Education*. New York: Basic Books.

Weigartner, Rudlph H. 1996. *Fitting Form to Function: A Primer on the Organization of Academic Institutions*. Phoenix, AZ: The Onyx Press.

White, Geoffrey D., and Flanner C. Hauck. 2000. *Campus, Inc.: Corporate Power in the Ivory Tower*. Amherst, NY: Prometheus Books.

Wildawksy, Ben. 2010. "How College Rankings Are Going Global (and Why Their Spread Will Be Good for Higher Education)" in Kevin Carey and Mark Schneider (eds.), *Accounting in American Higher Education*, 211–49. New York: Palgrave-Macmillan.

Wilke, Arthur S. 1979. "Preface." In Arthur S. Wilke (ed.), *The Hidden Professoriate: Credentialism, Professionalism, and the Tenure Crisis*, xi–xv. Westport, CN: Greenwood Press.

Wilson, John K. 2008. *Patriotic Correctness: Academic Freedom and its Enemies*. Boulder, CO: Paradigm Publishers.

Worthen, Helena, and Joe Berry. 1999. *Conditional Faculty in Public Higher Education in Pennsylvania, Spring, 1999: Focus on the Community Colleges*. Harrisburg, PA: Keystone Research Center.

Zdziarski, Eugene L. II, Norbert W. Dunkel, J. Michael Rollo, and Associates. 2007. *Campus Crisis Management: A Comprehensive Guide to Prevention, Response, and Recovery*. San Francisco, CA: Jossey-Bass Publishers.

Zemsky, Robert, Gregory R. Wegner, and William F. Massy. 2005. *Remaking the American University: Market-Smart and Mission-Centered*. New Brunswick, NJ: Rutgers University Press.

Zima, Peter V. 2002. *Deconstruction and Critical Theory*. London: Continuum.

Zumeta, William. 2004. "State Higher Education Financing: Demand Imperatives Meet Structural, Cyclical, and Political Constraints." In Edward P. St. John and Michael D. Parsons (eds.), *Public Funding of Higher Education: Changing Contexts and New Rationales*, 79–107. Baltimore, MD: The Johns Hopkins University Press.

Index

academia, status of, 8–9

academic administration: accretion and, 58–66; college/university ranking and, 68–69; as constituency, 50; increases in staff, 18; language and imagery of corporatism and, 90–91; as Parkinsonian, 60; professionalization of, 58–59; role of president, 63–64; shared governance and, 64–66, 65; structural alternative to, 60–64; as threat to academic culture, 59

academic capitalism, commercialization of higher education and, 98

Academic Capitalism (Slaughter & Leslie), 59

academic community, decline of, 38–39

academic culture, administration as threat to, 59

academic departments: competition among, 74; creation of, 15; difficulty in eliminating, 21, 23; discipline-based, 22–28; expansionist tendencies of, 24–25; organized research units as distraction from, 27–28; salary schedules and, 67; silo-ization within, 38; structure and culture of, 26–27; weakness of chair, 25–26 *See also* disciplines

academic freedom, ancillary faculty and, 111–14

academic presses, 17

academic stratification, accretion and, 66–77

academic tenure: ancillary faculty and, 110–11; as barrier to elimination, 20; economizing and, 95–96

access, minority students and, 83–84

accomplishments, of higher education, 5, 6

accountability, education and, 45–46, 81, 85–89; autonomy *vs.*, 80; commercialization of higher education and, 99; criticism of methodology, 87–88; tenure and, 96

accountability mania, 33

accreditation, for-profit institutions and, 104

adjunct faculty. *See* ancillary faculty

administration. *See* academic administration

administrative bloat, 60

admission standards, student consumerism and, 92

advertising institutions in media, 92

133